An
INDELIBLE EVENT
AND DETOUR
through a
GLOBAL
CHILDHOOD
A Memoir

HENRY M. SILVERT

CONTENTS

To Morrie, My Soul Mate and the Love of My Life

PREFACE

For days, I sat and stared at my computer screen, wondering how I was going to find the information I sought. Morrie, my wife, suggested Googling it. Yes, but which search words to use? The matter gnawed at me as I went about my daily life. Then, the answer suddenly announced itself in a dream. At 7:30 the next morning, my adrenaline rushing, I turned on the computer and searched "New Orleans newspapers."

I thought that if the information would be anywhere, it would be in the archives of one of the city's newspapers, however the list of links was a long one. Which one to choose first? Instead of overthinking it, I asked myself which newspaper would most likely contain the information I wanted. The most rational click was the newspaper I knew best. My only concern was that the records might have disappeared during Hurricane Katrina. Luckily, I hit the jackpot on my first try! I was shocked to find the article smack in the middle of the front page of the Saturday, June 4, 1955 *Times Picayune*. It was only ten extremely short paragraphs but contained all the information I had sought for so long. Squeezed next to stories about executions in San Quentin and an article about a knife fight involving a university football player was an article titled "Tulane Student Dies in Mexico." The article provided details about an automobile accident a few hundred miles north of Mexico City that involved a professor, his son, and two graduate students. It said that the car had "collided with a truck and rolled down" into a ravine. The article noted that the Tulane professor, who was not seriously injured and was able to call his wife, "was appointed recently as a member of the American Universities Field Staff and was to begin research on Guatemala and other Central American countries." The others in the car did not fare as well. The student who was driving lost his life, and the student sitting next to him and the boy stretched out sleeping on the backseat sustained severe head injuries.

The Times-Picayune

NEW ORLEANS, SATURDAY, JUNE 4, 1955

Two 'Professional Killers,' Woman Are Put to Death

TULANE STUDENT DIES IN MEXICO

Auto Accident Fatal to Igor Boussel

Word was received at Tulane university Friday of the death in Ciudad Valles, Mexico, of Igor Boussel, 23, Tulane graduate student, in an automobile accident Thursday.

Injured in the accident were Henry Silvert, 7-year-old son of Dr. and Mrs. Kalman Silvert of New Orleans, and Miss Marvelle Venetia Burris of Aberdeen, Wash., also a Tulane graduate student.

Dr. Silvert, who is an associate professor of political science at Tulane, was uninjured. His son was seriously injured. Mrs. Silvert left by plane for Mexico Friday afternoon.

Valles is about 300 miles northeast of Mexico City on the main Laredo tourist highway.

"I was not seriously hurt," Dr. Silvert told The Associated Press in Mexico. "I have contacted my wife in New Orleans, and she is coming here as fast as she can."

The AP reported that the car Boussel was driving collided with a truck and rolled down a ravine.

Dr. Silvert and the two students were en route to Guatemala, where they were scheduled to conduct research. Dr. Silvert was appointed recently as a member of the American Universities Field Staff and was to begin research on Guatemala and other Central American countries for the staff.

Boussel and Miss Burris were to conduct research for their masters' degrees.

Boussel, who was studying at Tulane under the auspices of the Institute of International Education, was from Paris. He is survived by his mother, Mrs. Andre Boussel of Paris.

Boussel was a graduate of Oxford university, England. He lived at 838 Lowerline.

Tulane Player Knifed in Fight

SHREVEPORT, La., June 3 (AP)— A Tulane football player and a

Three Go to Gas Chamber After Ordeal of Delays

By HAROLD V. STREETER

SAN QUENTIN, Calif., June 3 (AP)—Two professional killers and a pretty woman who got mixed up in one of their many murders died in San Quentin Prison's gas chamber today after an ordeal of last-minute legal delays.

Barbara Graham, whose love of money led to murder, died protesting the two futile stays that kept her alive an extra hour and a half. "Why do they torture me?"

Jack Santo and Emmet Perkins, convicted of six murders, died as easily as they had killed — chatty and almost debonair.

All three were executed for the robbery-murder of a Burbank, Calif., widow.

Mrs. Graham, 32, was pronounced dead at 11:42 a. m.

Other Murders Recalled

The husky Santo, 54, and his sidekick, Perkins, 47, were executed together three hours later. The San Quentin gas chamber seats but two and had to be aired for removal of Mrs. Graham's body before her companions could follow.

Besides the murder of Mrs. Mabel Monahan in 1953, they were under death sentences for the grisly massacre of a grocer and three little children in 1952, and under life terms for killing a gold miner in 1951.

Santo and Perkins were professional robbers who counted murder as part of their trade.

Mrs. Graham, 32, was a woman whose trade was sex—until she joined Santo and Perkins in the Monahan murder, a killing that profited none of them a penny.

One scant hour before her sched-

Continued on Page 3, Column 4

Employes Nar

Reprinted with permission from *The Times-Picayune | The New Orleans Advocate*

I was that boy, and I was not yet seven years old. My father Kalman was the professor. This article was a bonanza for me. It matched the little that my parents had told me and added a few interesting details about the accident's location. Before the accident, I was, according to my parents, an ornery, creative, precocious, and somewhat nerdy kid. I especially enjoyed playing the violin, which I started learning at the age of three, and playing contract bridge with my friends after rough games of hide-and-seek and tag. The accident changed all that.

I lost all memory of everything that had come before. Because I didn't know which skills I had acquired before the accident, once I remastered the basics, I took most things in stride. I let other people teach me the things that they thought I should know at the speed they thought appropriate. I was a blank slate absorbing people's input because I had no other knowledge to counter theirs. Recuperation was a long, tedious, exasperatingly slow, frustrating, and seemingly never-ending process. Looking back, these many decades later, I can see how the insistence of my parents and two brothers, Benjamin (Benjie) and Alexander (Ali), that I could do anything I set my mind to, kept me on the steady path toward improvement.

At the start of the relearning process, I had no choice but to do what I was told. "No" was not initially part of my vocabulary, and even after I learned and started using the word, those helping me would continue to nag, nag, nag until I invariably succumbed. In the end, even though the struggle to reinvent myself was at times a dauntingly painful and long chore, I also found the experience joyful and exhilarating. Despite the accident, or perhaps because of it, I focused on the possibilities of things not yet achieved rather than on the difficulties of realizing them. It was tedious learning how to walk and run again, but it was thrilling to eventually dance and play football, basketball, and table tennis. Ultimately, I was able to learn to play the violin and bridge again, but first I had to master what had been taken for granted: sitting up, talking, and comprehending what was said to me, as well as eating with utensils, reading, writing, and simply being able to think.

Some kids and adults teased me because I limped, my eyes were crooked, and my speech was slow and choppy. To my mind, they were shallow and rigid. By taking this attitude, I developed a stubbornness that empowered me to perceive the immense possibilities of life's beauty. The constant reminders from my tormentors that I was different and the continual conflict that it caused within me resulted in a type of force field that I built around myself. This impenetrable shield protected me from the naysayers, the teasers, and the bullies. Whenever someone managed to dent this protective layer with evil words, deeds, or a fistfight, my family was always around to help me. My perceptions of myself, of my small circle of friends, and of the world in general were framed in large part by the ways my family shielded me from the negativity of those who asserted that I would never amount to anything. To their credit, my parents never gave up their hope—*su esperanza*—that I could overcome many of the limitations that the accident caused. From the start, both of them were extremely obstinate toward those who said I would never even recover from a vegetative state.

Stubbornness runs deep in my family, and my parents were not going to give up on their dreams for my future. My father's persistence was subtle and largely directed toward my intellectual development, while my mother had an unyielding and adamant belief that I could do whatever people told her I couldn't. Even my brothers, although I wouldn't learn about it until years later, defended me against high school bullies. In the end, my father's continued encouragement, my mother's defiant attitude, and my brothers' protection helped me break free.

The accident itself, however, remained a relative mystery until I found the *Times Picayune* article. Both my parents apparently felt that it was better not to utter a word about the details of the accident to me in fear that I might be too traumatized. Maybe it was because they were the ones who were too traumatized. I did not know until my mother told me in September 2001, shortly before her death, that, until he died in June 1976, my father carried a great deal of guilt for the accident.

My childhood was also marked by the many places we lived. My circle of friends was constantly changing because we were always on the move from one country and city to another. We would live in a city for a year or year and a half, I would make some friends, and then we would move to another city where I repeated the entire process. Even if it was hard to make lasting friendships, I learned about different places, different cultures, different histories, and different cuisines. When I entered junior high school in Hanover, New Hampshire, I encountered a new set of issues, which stemmed from adjusting to a small, insulated community rather than the large city environment to which I'd become accustomed.

Wherever we lived, I don't remember ever meeting or seeing anyone, outside of a hospital or clinic, with any of my challenges, although undoubtedly, there had to have been people with similar and much worse conditions. It appeared that people with disabilities either voluntarily or forcefully stayed out of the public. As a result, whenever I encountered the world's wrongs—poverty, discrimination, segregation, bigotry, war, or inequality—I always identified with the underdog. I began to understand the world, or at least my world, as being composed of a series of overlapping, sometimes conflicting identities that fed my desire to resolve these injustices. These identities stemmed from overcoming the stigmas others placed on my limitations and finding a way that everyone could have a better life. The journey I took was a wild one and included everything from haggling in a philatelist's trading park in Buenos Aires and horseback riding lessons in Uruguay to Civil Rights and Vietnam War protests in the United States.

Since a person's life can't be adequately understood through a chronological ordering of events, I've told my story through various themes. The accident wasn't the beginning of my life, but it was and continues to be the most defining influence of my existence. Other facets of my identity have predominated and then subsided in my life at different times. I have tried, as best I can, to present my memories of these identity shifts and how they shaped me without too much interpretation. Memories, however, are always a reconstruction of the past from the point of view of the present. My current identity is informed by an optimistic—perhaps too optimistic—view of life as full of boundless opportunities.

EXPLORING FAMILY

Frieda and Kalman

In addition to being my protectors and mentors, my parents were fascinating people. While they could be extremely argumentative and assertive, they always sought to engage everyone, even those with whom they disagreed, and were eager to test their ideas. I don't remember a day in our home without a heated discussion of one kind or another with friends, students, or just other family members. We argued about the differences between democracy, authoritarianism, and fascism; efforts to lessen the prevalence of income and wealth inequalities in the United States and abroad; strategies to decrease the incidence of prejudice and discrimination in the United States and elsewhere in the world; and the need to empower people to be able to empathize with others. Everyone was welcome to contribute their views, and often voices were raised to accentuate a point, but we never stopped talking. My parents' views were not static, but rather were modified constantly by new information that evolved in current events, literature, and social scientific research. Instead of being frustrated, they became giddy when their perceptions were changed as a result of their research.

For example, my father and mother relished how their research indicated that people's perception of the role of formal education was determined by a number of influences, including their income, wealth, occupation, and political persuasion, rather than by a uniform view of education held by every member of society. For the following month, when they were not writing about this finding, my parents were consumed with discussing it with their colleagues and students and, more importantly, enjoying each other's company as they did so. It was not by chance that my parents exhibited traits of persistence, insistence, and stubbornness in their academic life and personal relations. They had acquired these attributes directly from their own families. Although both sets of my grandparents came to this country during the pogroms, their perceptions of the "American dream" differed greatly between the two sides of our family. My father's family focused more on entrepreneurship, while my mother's family devoted their efforts to political and intellectual pursuits. Despite these differences, both families were dedicated to succeeding in their new home country.

* * *

HENRY AND IDA

I never had the chance to meet my father's parents, who died more than a decade before I was born. In the prologue to his last book, *The Reason for Democracy*, published posthumously by The Viking Press in 1977, my father paid them an eloquent tribute:

> *In 1893 my parents came to this golden land. The metal they sought was not in mountains, in the beds of streams, or in banks. What drove them was the need to escape from tyranny into the sun of freedom. They knew that they were fated to carry*

the old ways into the new, that their acceptance in America would be hampered by themselves as well as by their hosts. It was through their children that they hoped the fulfillment of the American experience would be realized, their own migration made complete.

The stories my father talked about his parents' successes and failures were warm and filled with both riveting and sorrowful events that made me feel as if they were in the room and he was speaking directly with them. Henry and Ida started a custom-made furniture business in Bryn Mawr, Pennsylvania, shortly after arriving from Odessa, Ukraine. They thought the best way to advertise the quality of their craftsmanship and build the family's status in the community was to display several luxury cars outside their factory doors. And they spent an inordinate amount of time and money searching for the most appropriate cars to purchase. Every day, they would park two or three of these cars—a Lincoln Continental, a Packard, or a Jaguar—along the street next to their warehouse. Someone from the family would often drive the cars to prospective clients' homes. Automobiles were the way that my father's parents demonstrated to others their ethos of living the American dream. However, to Henry and Ida, the American dream meant more than simply the accumulation of wealth or material objects. It meant a strong work ethic and sharing your good fortune with others. Ida ran a small antique business out of their home where she sold many items on a "pay-when-you-can" basis for buyers short on cash.

Life was not always easy, and tragedy hit their furniture business twice. Shortly before the Great Depression, the warehouse and all its contents burned to the ground when someone carelessly flicked a partially extinguished match next to a can of turpentine. The fire also burned all of their cash because they kept it all in drawers scattered throughout the factory since they had no trust in banks. My grandparents had to sell their entire collection of cars to cover family expenses. There was, however, no question about whether to rebuild the furniture business. Their overwhelming quest for the American dream of rags to riches did not allow them to do anything but start over. And start over they did, and with a vengeance. They slowly rebuilt the factory and began to buy cars again. They also opened a bank account and dutifully made regular deposits.

Sadly, tragedy struck again when the factory burned to the ground a second time. This time though, Henry and Ida took consolation in the knowledge that their money was safe in a bank. Or so they thought until they discovered their bank declared bankruptcy a few days before the fire. There was no money to be had, and they had lost everything again! This must have left them devastated because they died shortly after the second fire. Although I don't know the exact cause of their deaths, heartbreak at having lost much of their wealth twice must have contributed to it.

* * *

ALEXANDER AND DORA

My mother's father and mother, Alexander and Dora Moskalik, were born in Pinsk, Belarus. They immigrated to the United States shortly after the pogroms in the early 20th century and lived in Philadelphia. Alex was a dentist, although he had pursued rabbinical studies before he arrived in the United States. When my mother spoke about her parents, one of her most cherished memories was the time Alex couldn't find his way to work one day. He was fluent in Russian and Yiddish, but did not speak, read, or write English well. To get to work, he would walk down the stairs from their second-story apartment, turn left, and then walk the three blocks until he saw a store sign with a picture of a Native American. Then he would turn left at the next corner and continue walking for two blocks until he arrived at his office. One day, he walked down the stairs, turned left, and walked, and walked, and walked, before realizing that he had missed the sign. So, he turned around, to retrace his steps back to the apartment. He repeated this process a number of times until he finally figured out that the sign had been taken down. He then asked his eldest daughter (my mother) to help him find his way to work. Alex died of a heart attack in 1955, the same year as my accident in Mexico and that my brother, Benjie, was born.

Dora was the only one of my grandparents I got to know quite well. Like Alex, she spoke Russian and Yiddish. She and Alex spoke these languages when they didn't want my mother or her sister, Nora, who we always called Bubbie (Yiddish for grandmother), to understand what they were saying. According to my mother, this forced her and her sister to learn a little Yiddish. Unlike Alex, however, Dora had a good command of English. I loved Dora, and thought she was highly intelligent and insightful. I would spend hours listening to her stories about the old country and her life in Philadelphia. We would often draw pictures and sing songs together. However, to say that she was a little bit on the wild side would be an understatement. My mother told me about a time when she was a teenager and Dora overheard her and her friends organizing a political rally. Dora disagreed with how they were using the word *bourgeoisie*. She entered the room and started walking around and around the table where the group was sitting, until my mother asked her angrily what the matter was. In the ensuing discussion, Dora took out the *Encyclopedia Britannica* and started reading aloud the part on the word in question, and when she realized it didn't say what she thought was right, she ripped the entire section from the book and stormed out of the room.

I had similar encounters with my grandmother. One that stands out because it exemplifies her insightfulness and tenacity occurred in Lovelady's Harbor, a town on Long Beach Island, New Jersey. Bubbie and my uncle Theodor, whom we called Teddy, had a summer place there. Dora and my family were visiting for a long weekend. There were not enough bedrooms, so my brother, Benjie, and I slept in the living room. Saturday morning, my brother and I were awakened at six in the morning by shouting and the bang of a suitcase hitting the floor. I went into the study and asked Teddy, whose routine was to get up every morning at five and work for a few hours on whatever book or article he was writing,

"What's happening?"

He replied, "Oh, it's just the normal. Your grandmother saw that the neighbors are going fishing this morning and asked them to take her to the bus at eight because she wants to go back to Philadelphia. But I told her that I would take her to the bus and that she should go back and tell the neighbors that she didn't need a ride."

"Why did she want to go back to Philly? She just got here yesterday," I said.

"I don't know why. She got upset about the conversation that you and Benjie had with her last night."

This was what always happened, except her anger was usually directed at adults. I said, "Why don't I drive her to the bus so that you can continue working?" I had an ulterior motive; I had just gotten my license to drive and no one in my family would let me drive while they were in the car. Teddy told me to go and ask her whether that would be okay. When I did, her reply was, "Okay, if I am not important enough for Teddy to take me himself." She assured me that she knew how to get to the bus stop, so we got into the car and off we went. When we were on the island's main road, she turned and started telling me the synopsis of a story by Isaac Loeb Peretz "Bontshe Shvayg" ("Bontshe: The Silent") in Russian.

She then asked, "Do you understand what I'm saying?" She did these kinds of things often.

I replied, "No, I don't understand Russian."

She said, "Okay! You're not cultured. I will tell it to you again."

She repeated the story in Yiddish this time and asked, "Now, you understand, don't you?"

"No, I don't understand Yiddish either."

"You see, you're not cultured. I will tell it to you again."

This time she told it to me in English, and then asked, "Do you know what the moral to the story is?"

Of course, I did. I had heard her tell the story and its moral many other times, but I said, "No."

She continued, "Well you see, the moral of the story is that all good things will come in good time."

At that point, we had passed the bus stop and reached the end of the island.

I said, "You don't know where the bus stop is, do you?"

She responded, "No, let's go back home."

Nobody was surprised when we both arrived back at the house. Her anger with the conversation the night before had subsided, and I was happy that I'd had the chance to drive a car!

* * *

NORA AND TEDDY

The belief among many that their country's values is superior to those of other countries has bothered me for years. My travels in Latin America and Europe, my experiences in New Orleans; Hanover, New Hampshire; and Norwich, Vermont, as well as my work on the Civil Rights and anti-war movements solidified my optimism that people can overcome ethnocentrism in this country and hopefully throughout the world. Clearly, today's politics make it evident that we have a long way to go.

My first contact with the concept of ethnocentrism came early in life, long before I ever heard the term. I met some boys when we lived in Buenos Aires and told them that I was from America, they promptly replied that they were from America, too. (See section "Making Friends" for the full story and its outcome.) Their comment hit home: America is a continent and not just a country. This anecdote has always been a clear and persistent reminder that we all need to understand the outlook and customs of those outside our cultural framework. To this day, I cringe whenever I hear a politician, an academic, or anyone else, whether they are from my country or not, refer to the United States as *America*. First, because there are many countries in America, and second, because the population of this country is diverse and contains within its borders many different cultures still in the process of assimilation. While I agree there is and always has been a dominant cultural framework in this country, I would argue that it is constantly being altered and modified by new ideas and behaviors brought here by immigrants.

My firm belief that the borders of the United States do not contain the entire continent and its people—and that its name should be distinguished from that of its neighbors—has often landed me in a heap of trouble. Many of my academic instructors lowered my grade on research papers when I argued this point. I also met with resistance from colleagues, whether in academia or in other professional endeavors, such as during the many years I spent at The Conference Board (TCB). For instance, while at TCB, I was a proponent of tailoring surveys to the nuances of local language, believing that the respect shown for respondents would increase the response rate. Most of the time, I didn't get too far and was told that everyone in the United States of America understands what is meant by this reference to our country.

I even encountered pushback when I expressed these views to my relatives, and inadvertently started a family feud about this issue. My mother, Bubbie, and Teddy, had rented a condominium in Great Barrington, Massachusetts, during the summer so they could attend concerts at Tanglewood and other nearby venues. My wife Morrie and I visited one weekend, and after dinner, Teddy and I were sitting on the sofa as I excitedly told him about the sociology class I was teaching. I began to explain how during the last class we were discussing difficulties with the concept of America. I didn't get too far into my story before Teddy became infuriated. His face turned a bright shade of red and he shouted, "You are brainwashing your students! America is great. I fought for America and for all it stands for during World War II. Don't be like your mother!" My mother, with Bubbie following right behind, came rushing out of the bedroom to defend me. After that I was not able to get another word into the conversation. Bubbie, Teddy, and my mother yelled at each other over their disagreements about authoritarianism, Stalinism, Trotskyism, Marxism, and democracy. They ignored Morrie and me when we tried to interject.

I probably should have been more empathetic and tried to understand Teddy's vehement opposition to what I had said, but it was difficult because his arguments with my mother had been going on for decades. They always followed the same pattern. There would be a lot of shouting for about 15 or 20 minutes and then the three of them would—little by little—start talking more calmly about other things, as if they had run out of gas. Then they'd go out to a movie, dinner, or a concert, have a good night's sleep and start up with a new argument some time the next day. This cycle was repeated daily when they were together, and they seemed powerless to stop it. My brothers and I usually steered clear of them during these outbursts. Although we didn't know for sure, I think that Teddy and my mother's disagreements were due to their long-standing political and ideological differences. Beginning in her teens until her mid-twenties, my mother was a member of the Communist Party of the United States (CPUSA), while Teddy belonged to the rival Trotskyist Party. At the time, each party was vying for the hearts and minds of people on the left. My mother ultimately resigned from the CPUSA because she didn't agree with its turn toward Stalin and the assassination of Leon Trotsky. However, she always remained a staunch Marxist, while Teddy became a rabid anti-Marxist. I don't quite understand how Teddy's political views could switch so completely, but I later observed the same transformation with one of my PhD advisors.

Although the argument in Great Barrington veered away from the original dispute, the main point of contention was Teddy's assertion that ethnocentrism and a love of one's country were one and the same. I don't think this is accurate. A person can disagree with certain policies or ideologies of his or her own country and still love it, or rather disagree with some things about other countries and not be ethnocentric. Teddy's rant did not give credence to the validity of any ideas emanating from any country but his own. Despite my disagreements with Teddy, I miss hearing those debates, and the arguments continue to resonate in my mind.

* * *

FRIEDA

Frieda

As might be expected, my mother started my political education early. The first song that she taught me after the accident started like this,

> *One, two, three, pioneers are we*
> *We're fighting for the working class, against the bourgeoisie*
> *We're going to teach our teachers a new philosophy.*
> *The workers own one-third of the world. That's pure geography.*

She told me she'd learned it as a teenager in summer camp.

My mother was also a supporter of the fight against Francisco Franco during the Spanish Civil War, although she didn't fight in Spain. She had been a member of the Communist Party of the United States, but, as I've mentioned, quit because she thought the party was wrong in supporting the anti-Marxist authoritarian policies of Joseph Stalin. Along with many other defectors from the party, she argued this was the only way to remain a Marxist. When I read Jorge Semprun's *Autobiography of Federico Sanchez*, about his participation in the Spanish Civil War, I found his arguments on the topic strikingly similar to my mother's.

Like her mother before her, my mother wasn't afraid to express her opinions, no matter the occasion or setting, and here is the perfect example. For many years, my father worked as a special adviser for Latin America at the Ford Foundation in New York City. One day, without his knowledge, his secretary accepted an invitation for him from Vice President Hubert Humphrey's office to a dinner for the President of Mexico. When my father heard about this, he was surprised, but told his secretary to inform the Vice President's office that my mother would also be attending. When my parents arrived at the dinner, they ran into some colleagues and assumed they would be sitting with them. Instead, they were seated at the table with Humphrey, his wife, and the President of Mexico and his wife. When the entrées arrived, my mother turned to Vice President Humphrey and asked, "So, when are we going to get out of Vietnam?" The table went silent. I think that this was exactly what my father wanted and expected my mother to do. When they returned to New York, both my mother and father told me that Humphrey's reaction was to point out the necessity of fighting against communism.

My mother was just as candid and forthright with her friends, with whom she often engaged in heated conversations. Although she always supported her position with facts, she felt many of her friends didn't take her seriously because they held advanced degrees and she didn't. She later told me that every time she was about to enter graduate school, she would get pregnant. She was eventually able to fulfill this lifelong dream at the age of 58 when she received her doctorate from the University of Bremen in Germany.

KALMAN'S PATH TO NEW ORLEANS

Kal in the army

Prejudice and discrimination also played a large role in my father's choice about which field of study to pursue in graduate school and why he landed at Tulane University. When he completed his undergraduate studies at the University of Pennsylvania, my father was among those who received a very low number in the 1942 military draft lottery. There were 365 chits, each with a month and a day signifying a person's birthday, which were drawn randomly from a bowl. People with birthdays on chits that were drawn at the beginning of the process were more likely to be called for military service than those whose chits were pulled later. My father's chit was the first one picked. He was posted in Kenya in the Army's Air Force division because, he told me, he was fluent in Swahili and Arabic.

After the war, my father initially entered the anthropology graduate program at the University of Pennsylvania, but soon realized that he had serious philosophical and theoretical differences with some of the more influential professors in his department. When he transferred to the Political Science Department, my father's advisor cautioned him that because of the political climate and the long-standing anti-Semitism and anti-intellectualism of this country's political elite, it would be best for him to specialize in a relatively unknown and distant region of the world. His advisor suggested Latin America as a general area of concentration, and Chile, one of the countries farthest from the United States, as a great place for his dissertation research.

My father learned to speak, write, and read Spanish before traveling to Santiago, Chile, with my mother, whom he had married three months earlier, in 1948. The university declared his 1949 dissertation on Chile's development corporation the top dissertation of the year, an honor usually accompanied by an offer of a teaching job. Again, because of the growing anti-intellectual and anti-Semitic political climate and the denunciation of free speech in Washington, D.C., the university had no intention of offering him this honor or providing guidance on other positions. It was only when one of the department secretaries surreptitiously slipped him an ad that he found out about the position at Tulane University.

The rampant segregation and discrimination in New Orleans eventually became too much for my mother and father to stomach. In the fall of 1958, while my father was preparing notes for his fall classes, he submitted a grant proposal to the Brookings Institution to conduct a study on the role that formal education played in the social, economic, and political development in Argentina, Brazil, Chile, and Mexico. He also actively looked for work at another university or college. While we were in Argentina, he was offered a full professorship at Dartmouth College in Hanover, New Hampshire.

BENJAMIN AND ALEXANDER

Ali, Benjie, and me

I always felt in competition with my brothers, and they probably felt the same way toward me. Both my brothers were much younger than me (Benjie by 6 years and Ali by 9 years). I was consumed with overcoming my physical and mental challenges, so we did not share many interests when we were young. While they could ski and play tennis and other sports together, my sports experience was mainly relegated to playing table tennis with my father. My brothers also liked to play table tennis, but they didn't have the patience needed to play with me.

My brothers also formed an early and unique bond through language when we moved to Hanover. Benjie quickly adapted to using English, but Ali, who had not yet quite learned to speak in either English or Spanish, insisted on communicating in a gobbledygook of his own creation. Benjie was the only one who understood Ali's new language and acted as his interpreter.

One morning, shortly after we arrived in Hanover from Buenos Aires, Ali took off to his nursery school down the block. When he returned at noon, my mother asked him why he wasn't in school. But she couldn't get a translation until Benjie returned from school later that afternoon. After hearing Ali's tale, Benjie explained to my mother that no one was at the school when Ali arrived. He'd climbed in through an unlocked window and started drawing pictures on paper. When he got hungry, he came home. It turned out that school had been cancelled for a teacher meeting, and Ali had not given my mother the note.

A LIFE-ALTERING ROAD TRIP

My memories of my early life immediately after the accident are very good. I remember it as a time of fun, adventure, and learning. It was an era in which I felt a sense of the intense and extreme generosity of other people toward me. Of course, the horrendous effects of the car wreck had a terrible and permanent influence on my childhood and my life. But I only realized this in hindsight. At the time, I was too busy being a kid and learning from experience to notice.

While I didn't understand it at the time, I would never have succeeded without the encouragement and help of those close to my family and even those who were not close at all. Beginning with the people of Ciudad Valles, where the accident took place, I have benefited again and again from the generosity of others.

After I was released from the hospital, most of this group—parents, teachers, doctors, friends, and tutors—encouraged me to overcome my limitations. In the end, all of these people gave me the freedom and space to make mistakes while I was learning.

ENTER PEPI

In June 1955, just five months shy of my seventh birthday and right after I completed first grade, my father and I started out on what was supposed to be a more than 2,200-mile car ride from New Orleans to Guatemala City. My father was beginning a year's sabbatical to enrich his understanding of Central American processes of social and political development. My mother would fly down with six-month-old Benjie shortly after we got there.

I threw a tantrum when my parents first told me about the trip. I didn't want to leave my friends in New Orleans to spend an entire year in Guatemala. There was no way I was going to go. Period! This defiant stance was my initial response throughout my childhood every time we had to leave one city for another, though my mother found an ingenious way to assuage my anxieties about our moves. With a soothing tone, she would remind me of all the stories I could tell my friends when I returned. To give me an idea of how much fun I would have, she would tell me an ongoing bedtime story about the adventures of Enrique (my name in Spanish) and his dog Pepi. She described in great detail how these two friends would cross fields, climb up mountains, explore Guatemala's pyramids, and build sandcastles on the country's Caribbean and Pacific beaches. Along with their adventures, Enrique and Pepi shared a secret. Pepi could talk, and the pair conducted elaborate conversations in English and Spanish. By telling these travel tales long before our journey began, my mother helped me forget all my fears about starting somewhere new. I loved these stories so much that memories of them lingered for many years, and I always looked forward to hearing a new chapter in their adventures before every trip we took.

HOW IT BEGAN

Two graduate students from Tulane University were joining us for the drive to Guatemala. Igor Boussel was a 23-year-old Parisian who, after having completed his undergraduate studies at the University of Oxford, was working toward his master's degree in anthropology. He planned to conduct research during the summer in the Mayan communities of Chichen Itza. Marvelle Venetia Burris, from Aberdeen, Washington, was also a student in the master's program in anthropology, and her research focus was on the culture of the indigenous population close to Guatemala City. A month or so before we set off from New Orleans, my father bought a used four-door silver and black Jaguar from a neighbor for the trip. Given his family's history with fancy cars, it's hardly a surprising choice. He had flirted with buying a Jaguar since he had joined the faculty at Tulane but purchasing a new one on an assistant professor's salary, even in 1955, was out of the question. He grudgingly settled for a used one.

When we were ready to leave, the Jaguar was packed to the hilt. In addition to several small suitcases filling the trunk of the car, there were two trunks and three suitcases full of clothes and books on the floor between the car's front and backseats; three typewriter cases stuck between the suitcases in front of the car's backseat; and bags of sweets and sandwiches between the two front bucket seats just behind the gear shaft. After my mother kissed and hugged me goodbye and said that she'd see me in a few days, we started on our journey. My father was driving, Igor was in the front passenger seat while Marvelle and I were sitting in back, squished between the books and the suitcases and excited to be heading to Guatemala.

Our route from New Orleans went halfway through Texas and then turned southward toward the Mexican border. After crossing the border, we were going to continue south along Route 82, hugging the coast of the Gulf of Mexico until we crossed into Guatemala, and then turn inland toward Guatemala City. As the daylight turned into evening shade about 400 miles north of Mexico City, my father pulled to the side of the road to let Igor take the wheel. My father and I laid down on the backseat and went to sleep.

When I woke up, I was no longer in the car or next to my father. I was in a single bed at the Central Military Hospital in Mexico City. On the outskirts of Ciudad Valles, Igor rammed our car straight into an oncoming truck. He was driving so fast that the Jag went all the way under the length of the truck, coming out at its tail end with the car's top smashed and almost completely sheared off. The car then fell into a ravine along the side of the mountain.

Several years later, while having dinner in New Orleans, my mother and father calmly told me that they later found out Igor had written a suicide note before we left New Orleans. I guess he'd decided that not only was our trip the best opportunity to carry out his plan, but he would also take all of us along for the ride. One part of his plan succeeded when he was killed instantaneously. Marvelle was badly injured and part of her scalp was sheared off, but she survived. My father fell out of the car when the back door swung open after the car came out from under the truck. His body ricocheted and skidded along the concrete and gravel of the road, leaving cuts on his cheeks very close to both of his eyes. I was later told that if the cuts had just been a little closer to his eyes, he would have lost all sight. He also had a busted left elbow. The Associated Press news item that I had found noted that my father hadn't sustained any serious injuries and was able to notify my mother of the accident.

I was hit right above my left earlobe by one of the hard-cased suitcases, which had bounced up from the car's floor as both the car and I tumbled down the mountainside into a ravine.

I gleaned these details of the accident over many, many years of listening carefully to what little my parents shared with me. Initially, all they told me was that one student had died in the accident. I didn't even learn Igor Boussel's name until I read that newspaper article online 65 years later. I'm not sure whether it would have made any difference if I had been told about this earlier. Perhaps I was not told because I wasn't curious enough to press for details and never asked? Or were they simply too involved in making sure that I recovered sufficiently enough to lead a semi-normal life? I will never know the answer because both of my parents died long ago.

* * *

FILLING IN THE BLANKS

Joel

As luck or fate would have it, I recently discovered new details about the accident and confirmation of some other things that I already knew. Morrie and I were having dinner with Joel and Betty Jutkowitz, longtime friends of my family. After taking several of my father's classes as an undergraduate at Dartmouth College, Joel had followed in his footsteps as a specialist in Latin American studies, writing his doctoral dissertation on Chile. He had also been one of my father's graduate students at New York University. He met and married Betty while conducting research for his doctoral dissertation and working at the United Nations Economic Commission for Latin America and the Caribbean in Santiago. Joel, Betty, and I became close friends when I lived at their house in Santiago during the summer of 1972 while conducting my own research on Chile's commitment to democratic processes for my bachelor of philosophy degree at the University of Oxford in England (see section, "A Return to Santiago).

Until our recent meeting, I had no idea how much Joel knew about the accident. During dinner, he launched into a detailed account and how he had learned about it. One weekend during his junior year at Dartmouth, he was in a quandary about how to deliver an important paper to a friend at Harvard. He knew we had two cars, so Joel asked my dad if he could borrow our convertible Lincoln Continental. (As with the Jag, my father bought the Lincoln used for only $1,500 from a neighbor who had two Lincolns.) My father always found it extremely difficult to say no to anyone, especially one of his students, but Joel noticed a certain hesitation before my father agreed to the loan. Joel assured him that he was a very good driver. My father explained that Joel's driving wasn't what concerned him, but rather his memory of the terrible accident he'd had in Mexico a long time ago.

Kal sitting in the Lincoln

Joel had never heard about the accident before, and after a little prodding, my father told him everything. Joel said that it seemed that my father was anxious to talk about it. He confirmed that Igor had written a suicide note, and he also described how the people of Ciudad Valles, total strangers, poured out from their homes to assist in any way they could. When my father told them that I was still in the car, five men rushed down into the ravine to get me. When I heard about the selfless generosity of these individuals and other people in Ciudad Valles, I wondered whether, even though I was in a coma

22

at the time, I knew what was happening around me. Could this experience have been a major factor in my continuing optimism about life's possibilities?

After the townspeople rescued me from the ravine, they noticed I had a very high fever. A wealthy resident who owned one of the few cars with air conditioning volunteered and brought his car to the scene of the accident with the hope that the cool air would stabilize my fever. They placed me in the backseat and let the air conditioning do its work until the paramedics arrived. The car's battery charge lasted long enough for the paramedics to take over my care. Despite my father's offer, the owner of the car refused to accept any money to have the battery recharged.

A couple let my father use their phone to reach my mother. He had to place the call through the international operator, who stayed on the line throughout the call. After my father assured my mother that he had not been seriously hurt, they started to consider my condition. They had heard of a very successful teaching program at an institute in Chicago to train Mexican physicians in neurological science and surgery and thought that facility could assist in finding a doctor in Mexico.

My parents didn't know the name of the institute or a doctor in Chicago who might know the name. The international operator, who was silently listening to the conversation, said that she could set up a three-way conversation with someone at the University of Chicago Medical Center who might be able to assist. The operator spent about 15 minutes speaking with the main switchboard operator at the university before locating a person who could suggest a neurosurgeon in Mexico. The Chicago doctor gave Dr. Manuel Sanchez-Garibay his highest recommendation. The operator found the doctor's phone number in Mexico City and patched him into the call.

DR. MANUEL SANCHEZ-GARIBAY

Manuel, Beulah, Frieda, and Kal

Manuel, who was to play a major role in my recovery, was the head of the Neurosurgery Department at the Military Hospital in Mexico City. In my father's interview with him, published by the American Universities Field Staff, I learned that Manuel's family had emigrated from Spain a few years before the start of the 1910 Mexican Revolution. While his family's financial means were modest compared to U.S. standards, his father had owned and managed a chain of bakeries in Mexico City until the late 1930s. When it was time for Manuel to go to university, his parents urged him to enter the military so that the army would finance his medical education. He graduated from the Mexican Military Medical School in 1938 and interned with a rural practice until 1940. In 1944, the army offered him a scholarship to continue his medical studies at the Illinois Medical Institute in Chicago, and in 1948, he became the first Mexican surgeon to receive certification from the American Board of Neurological Surgery. Manuel met and married Beulah, a native Chicagoan who worked as a nurse at the time. He was a workaholic and was also on the staff of two other hospitals, a full professor at two universities in Mexico City, and served as a medical consultant for the Mexican railway system. At the time of the accident, he was a colonel in the Mexican Army but later worked his way up to lieutenant general.

After my mother and father explained their reason for calling, Manuel's immediate assessment of my medical condition was extremely negative. He warned that there was only an infinitesimal likelihood for my survival. He was reluctant to become involved, but my parents implored him to at least come to Ciudad Valles, examine me in person and appraise my chances. I think that Manuel's scientific curiosity along with his penchant for challenging cases got the better of him. That along with a little nudging from his wife Beulah and my mother's persistence convinced him to agree to have a look at me.

My mother met Manuel at the airport in Mexico City and they drove to Ciudad Valles. When they arrived at the clinic, he first checked on my father's condition. After determining that my father's injuries were not extremely serious, Manuel turned his attention to me and asked the local doctors for their diagnosis. They told him that my condition appeared to be hopeless and they didn't think that any heroic actions would succeed. Therefore, they thought that the best solution was to declare me dead and bury me. However, Manuel's initial skepticism about my chances for survival changed because I had not yet succumbed to death.

My parents told me later that after Manuel examined me, he turned to them and exclaimed, "This boy doesn't know how to die!" He knew the local clinic could not provide the necessary medical care and so told my parents that he wanted to transfer me to the Military Hospital in Mexico City as his nephew, since only military personnel and their families were permitted. As compensation for his trip to Ciudad Valles, he accepted the smashed, unrecognizable Jaguar.

* * *

SMALL STEPS TOWARD RECOVERY

During the two-month period that I started regaining consciousness, everything was a mystery. I kept waking up and nodding back to sleep. Where had all my energy gone? Who were the strangers in my room? Why was everyone making such a fuss over me? What were they saying? Why couldn't I move, hear, talk, or get out of bed? Where was I? Where was my father?

Why couldn't I open my right eyelid? I was confused and frustrated because my memory was incomplete. I remembered a few things, just not very well or very clearly. I had no recollection of the accident. I knew my father and I were traveling somewhere without my mother, but I had no inkling of where we were going or what had come before. (Scenes from that time would return to my memory later.)

I made up stories in my head to answer these questions. One was that my father had carried me from the car to a hotel room. But where was he? We usually slept in the same room when traveling, but he wasn't there. In my waking moments, I tried, to no avail, to call out to him. In addition, during one of my brief periods of wakefulness, I noted that my bed had railings. Didn't he know that I was old enough not to need railings on my bed? Another time, I saw a man looking down at me wearing a strange looking uniform. Why would my father let a stranger into our hotel room? Whenever the strange man in the uniform was not next to my bed, my mother, with her smiling face, was always there. How had she found our hotel room? My initial answer was she must have stuck herself into a cardboard pack of Winston cigarettes and floated in the air. Not in a spiral fashion, but in a wobbly manner like a comet traveling through space. I saw this image whenever she appeared during my moments of wakefulness, although sometimes she traveled in a Winston matchbox (my parents' favorite brand of cigarettes) or one of those flip-top match containers.

My mother wasn't the only person coming in and out of my room. There was always someone talking to me, fretting over my rumpled sheets, taking my temperature, or simply just sitting and talking or reading a book or a newspaper to me. As I experienced longer periods of consciousness, I started to have other questions. While the sight in both of my eyes was very poor, why was the vision in my right eye much better than in my left? Why couldn't I move my right eyeball out of the corner of the socket, and why was it necessary to twist my head to look at people? Why couldn't I focus on anything with both eyes at the same time? All these questions left me frustrated more than angry or sad. I had no one to be angry toward, and sadness is a reflection of unhappy feelings about the past. While I had sporadic memories of the immediate past, I had no recollection of the more distant past, and no knowledge of the present. Anger would have to wait, and dejection was out of the question because I was barely aware of the present, the here and now.

Manuel told my parents that I was, in layman's terms, in a vegetative state and any amount of improvement would be entirely up to me. All they could do was "set the table for me" and wait and see how far I could or would go. Manuel counseled them, saying that those around me would have to be optimistic and supportive in every possible way. Patience would be a virtue. While he did not give up hope that my condition would improve over time, he could not say how much to expect or how long it would take. This must have been difficult for my parents to hear, however I think that, although trial and error factored in, they followed Manuel's advice.

* * *

LEARNING AND RELEARNING

Manuel also advised my parents that, although they would be tempted to do things for me, to whatever extent possible, I needed to take care of myself. He gave the same instructions to all the doctors and nurses. By forcing me to learn on my own, Manuel hoped I would become empowered and feel confident enough to face new challenges myself. Manuel's prescription didn't mean that the people around me had to be passive. Quite the contrary, he encouraged everyone to urge me to use the right side of my body so that the muscles would not continue to atrophy and would instead regain the ability to function. Later, he told my parents that I would often complain, scream, and refuse to master certain tasks because the process was long, tedious, and painful some of the time, and unpleasant and arduous most of the time. I eventually agreed to do everything. While the end result always made me happy and encouraged me to do more, during the process I was a grumpy kid. Because of Manuel's instructions, no one gave into my protestations and lamentations. Any time I yelled, "I don't want to do that," the staff would simply persist until I agreed.

Until well into my adulthood both my mother and father were like a broken record, constantly reminding me, "Swing your right arm when you walk. Use your right hand. Lift and bend your right leg. Don't drag your right leg." Their words still haunt me to this day when I walk.

This repetition was necessary for me to relearn basic life functions as quickly as possible. In addition to emphasizing positive reinforcement, Manuel instructed the doctors, nurses, and interns to teach me how to do things independently.

Determined and patient, Nurse Maria taught me how to eat with a fork and a knife. This task was extremely difficult because of the weakness and near paralysis in my right arm and hand. I was taught to eat Mexican style. I later discovered that manner of eating was also common throughout Latin America and in most of the world, but not in the United States. In Mexico, the fork *stays* in the left hand and the knife remains in the right hand and is used to slice food and secure it to the fork, then the fork is brought to the mouth. This is even the case with food that doesn't require cutting. In the United States – for right-dominant people such as myself – after cutting food with a knife in the right hand and the fork in the left, it is customary to switch the fork to the right hand prior to eating.

Nurse Maria demonstrated and told me to imitate her. Because I could not yet understand either Spanish or English, I got the gist of what she wanted me to do from her hand gestures. I took the handle of the fork in my left hand parallel to my body, pointed the prongs downward, and with the knife in my right hand, also parallel to my body and with the sharp side pointed downward, I stuck the fork into a piece of meat. I then placed the knife on the meat, behind and parallel to the fork, and began moving the knife back and forth to cut the meat. This was not an easy process for me. I was frustrated when it didn't work the first few times and, because I was leaning on the propped upside of the bed, meat splattered all over. After many, many tries, I was finally successful.

Thanks to a special incentive, relearning Spanish comprehension was much more fun than learning to speak. Nurse Luz and Nurse Maria-Isabel, two beautiful women (or at least to my mind) sat on opposite sides at the head of my bed. When I looked at Luz, she would point to Maria-Isabel on the other side of the bed and say, "*Mira para ya*" (look that way). With a little coaxing, I got the point and turned my head to the nurse on the other side and was rewarded with a piece of chocolate. Then the nurse who gave me the chocolate pointed in the other direction and said to look back the other way. I did as I was told because I wanted more chocolate. This continued until they realized that I was turning my head before they even asked, which meant I was no longer listening to the words they were trying to teach me.

Learning to speak again was a little more difficult even though they used the same basic technique. One nurse would ask if I wanted a piece of chocolate, but when I started to turn, she stopped me and, signaling with her hands and using slow mouth movements for me to imitate, indicated that I should say, "*Si, yo quiero un pedaso de chocolate.*" Just as for a baby this was challenging, and it took a long time to figure out how to form the words so that they sounded right, but eventually I succeeded. As a result, the first language I learned after the accident was Spanish. There's no doubt that the tasty chocolate was my main incentive to comprehending and to *talking* again.

I was soon able to move a little better, though standing up straight and balancing on both feet was both difficult and painful. With the nurses' help, I'd roll over onto my left side, and using only my left hand, since I did not have the strength in the right one, I'd slowly push myself up into a sitting position. Then I'd move to the edge of the bed and swing my feet over the side. There was a step stool waiting to help me reach the floor from the high bed. One nurse held me to prevent me from falling to the side, backward, or even forward onto the floor. Using the stool was the easiest part as each nurse took one of my arms and held me steady, while I gingerly and clumsily stepped down to the floor. Once my feet firmly reached the floor, using a series of verbal commands and hand and body movements, the nurses said to stand still and upright, and distribute my weight equally on both feet. This was initially impossible because my right leg was so weak and my right foot so droopy. I tried to follow their directions as best I could. They next instructed me to take a step by lifting my left leg, bringing it forward, stepping down, and then doing the same with my right. I needed assistance when it came to my right side since I couldn't balance myself on my foot when the left one was in the air. Not to mention, as soon as I lifted my right leg, the foot would drop, and I had trouble moving my leg forward. I only took one step forward during the hour of the first walking lesson. That first time was a complete failure and I almost crumpled to the floor, but the nurses caught me and held me up. Over time, as I progressed, these sessions became easier.

* * *

HOSPITAL LIFE

Some doctors and nurses, especially the younger ones who weren't aware of Manuel's reputation, disagreed with his patient and cautious approach to my rehabilitation. One day before Manuel arrived at the hospital, I was sitting in a chair listening to my parents discuss Mexican politics when two young neurology residents entered. They said that my right foot and leg were not showing sufficient signs of improvement and the only remedy was to immobilize the entire leg in a cast. It was true that many of the muscles in my right leg had atrophied. In addition, my foot turned in and pointed downward at about a 60-degree angle from my ankle, and I could not move it actively, no matter how hard I willed it. It was not stiff and was really quite mobile if I moved it passively with my hand. It just wouldn't follow any commands coming from my brain.

My parents explained that Manuel had told them that a cast was not necessary and would only exacerbate my muscle atrophy. They implored the doctors to wait until Manuel arrived.

One of the doctors said, "No, you are not a doctor. Time is of the essence, and we must do it promptly."

My mother pleaded, "Manuel is expected to be here in an hour. Can't we wait until then?"

"No, it must be done immediately."

The residents momentarily won this battle of hospital politics, so off I went on a gurney to the cast department. I was fitted with a plaster cast that began halfway up my hip and ended just before my toes. Manuel was livid when he saw the cast and asked a nurse to summon the two residents. When they came in, using his most authoritative tone, Manuel loudly berated the two. "I am in command on this floor, and I must agree to any medical decisions concerning this patient." He then had two orderlies put me back on the gurney and take me to have the cast removed. All I thought was I get to have another ride on the gurney! I am sure my parents were horrified, but moments of levity like this gave me a chance to relax.

* * *

FIRST STEPS: TAKE TWO

Even with these brief moments of humor, at least from my vantage point, the start of my recovery remained slow, arduous, and exasperating. I had no say about anything and could only follow what I was told or asked to do. The months I spent in the hospital were only the beginning of the process to recoup my physical abilities and mental awareness. However, after six months of being cooped up there, it was time to move on. Since my father had six months remaining on his sabbatical and could continue to conduct research and write on Central American politics in Mexico, we remained in Mexico City for my intensive outpatient physiotherapy. I called physiotherapy "physio-o-therapy" with a heavy accent on the "o" because I hated it so much. Today, it's generally known as physical therapy.

Before I could start this new chapter of my life though, I needed to pass another milestone. Walking out of the hospital was not an easy task. Usually, when someone is discharged from a hospital, he or she is pushed in a wheelchair to the front door and only permitted to stand once having crossed the threshold. But Manuel was vehemently against following this policy, he thought it might reinforce the idea that it was easier to get around in a wheelchair than to walk on my own two feet. As I'd already learned during the "cast" episode, whatever Manuel wanted, he got.

Right before I left, Manuel told me, "Don't worry if you fall. Just pick yourself up and continue walking. Nothing bad will happen to you. We'll be right next to you."

I said, "Okay," and slowly got off the bed and started to walk out of the room.

After a few steps, I fell, and the nurses, who had not heard Manuel's instructions, tried to help me up off the floor while soothing me. Manuel's signal stopped them in their tracks, and in a commanding voice, he said, "Leave him alone. He can do it by himself!" They backed off.

I repeated this process every two steps until I was in front of the 4th floor elevator. My parents and Manuel were hesitant to let me continue without a helping hand, but they refrained from interceding. In Spanish, Manuel said, "Hankie, push the down button." I understood and did so. By that time, I understood almost everything that was said in Spanish, but I still had a way to go in my English comprehension. We entered the elevator, and I was instructed to press the button for the lobby, which was labeled "PB" for the Spanish words "*Planta Baja.*" Once we reached the ground floor, the long walk down the main hallway to the front door seemed to take ages. The same sequence of tripping, getting up, people rushing to help, and Manuel telling them to leave me alone repeated itself. As soon as we emerged through the front door of the hospital, my father went to get the car. Once I was in the car, Manuel leaned down through the open door and said, "I am not going to give you crutches or a wheelchair to take home because I want you to do as much as you can on your own. Don't worry if you fall, and, if you need to, balance yourself using the furniture. I don't want you to be stopped from improving as much as you can by using anything but your natural surroundings and your own will. I will come to your house on Mondays, Wednesdays, and Fridays at six o'clock in the morning to take you to physiotherapy. Do you understand?"

I said that I did, but I really didn't understand the importance of what he was saying. Then, he said, "I'll pick you up next Monday morning. Bye!"

* * *

Frieda, Beulah, Hank, Benjie, and Isabel

MORNINGS WITH MANUEL

My parents had rented a two-story single-family house in a relatively upscale, largely residential section in the city called Polanco. All I remember was that there was a big couch in the middle of the living room that I held onto when I was walking around. As promised, Manuel came three times a week at six a.m. in one of his many cars to take me to the hospital for physical therapy sessions. (Like my father and his family, Manuel was a car-collecting fanatic!) The reason he came so early was that before arriving at the hospital, he would drive through some of the poorest neighborhoods of Mexico City to help those who needed medical attention but couldn't afford it. On the days that I was with him, I'd accompany him into people's homes and watch while he calmly treated those with illnesses ranging from common colds to broken bones.

One of these patients was a man in his thirties who was sitting, bent over, in a poorly lit room, and looked like he was in pain. A dirty, bloodstained piece of white sheet was wrapped around his upper left arm. Blood streamed down his arm to the tips of his fingers. I don't know how Manuel knew to stop at his house, because apparently the man had only been shot recently while he was walking home from buying groceries. How did he call for help when there wasn't even a telephone that I could see? Manuel told the man's wife in a firm but calm voice to boil some water and take a chair, a table, a pitcher with water, and a glass to the sunlit patio. Once they were settled on the patio, Manuel poured water into the glass and gave the man a painkiller. He took the makeshift dressing off the man's arm and gently cleaned the wound with the hot water and then poured alcohol over it. Once he had a clear view, Manuel said that he had to remove the bullet, which was still lodged in the man's arm. He did not carry any topical or local anesthetics with him, so he informed the man that it was going to hurt a great deal, but the pain would only last a short time. Before Manuel did anything, he asked me whether I would prefer to go out to the car and wait until he finished. Quite the contrary; I was intrigued. While the man screamed in agony, Manuel extracted the bullet and, after inspecting the area for further damage, put disinfectant on a bandage and wrapped it around the arm. He then said that he would return the next day to check the wound.

At another home, he performed a gynecological exam for a pregnant woman, and on a subsequent visit, delivered her baby girl. The woman's family surrounded her because this examination was done on the "public" patio. Of course, I was not permitted to watch but I heard Manuel's easygoing explanation of each thing he was doing.

As payment, Manuel would accept anything people were able to give, whether it was tortillas, fried beans, or just a simple "thank you." It didn't occur to me that other doctors would treat patients any differently from Manuel. Going to their homes when they didn't have the means to go to hospitals or clinics seemed like a natural part of "being a doctor." I was always fascinated with the care and the gentleness that he gave each person he saw.

No matter how many stops he made, we always arrived at Manuel's assigned hospital parking space at 10 a.m. sharp. I would rush from the parking lot, still falling occasionally, arriving a little late for my physiotherapy sessions. I hated the first part of those sessions because the therapists applied electrical stimulation to my entire body, which always left pockmarks for a few hours afterward. I would then work on exercises to strengthen the right side of my body. The last part of the sessions was my favorite. I'd change into my bathing suit and dip into the shallow, warm-water pool. As the water soothed my body, the therapist would massage my stiff legs and feet.

At the end of each physical therapy session, I'd go up to the 4th floor, which Manuel called "his floor." I'd go into the doctors' locker room and, put on the scrubs, gloves, a mask, and cap that Manuel had ordered made for me, and then head straight for the operating room where he was usually operating on a patient. Manuel had told the hospital administrators and my parents that I was going to be in the operating room. Somehow my parents agreed, though it must have seemed unorthodox. Manuel was the boss of the neurosurgery floor of the hospital and he always had the final say. After the day's operation, the two of us would return to the locker room, take a shower, get dressed, and eat lunch in his office. He then examined patients in his office while I sat in a corner and observed.

In one case, Manuel's patient was a young boy whose head was unnaturally enlarged in the area above his eyes and forehead. Manuel determined there was quite a bit of pus that had accumulated between the skull and the skin, and scheduled surgery for the following Wednesday. I attended the surgery and watched Manuel pump the pus out. It turned out not to be a major surgery since the pus wasn't under any bones. Manuel made a small incision in the skin at the top of the boy's shaved head and inserted what looked like the nozzle of a bicycle pump. He then used its handle to pump the pus out from under the skin, which fell into a container on the floor. I was overwhelmed and surprised that a simple pump could be used to such an end.

In another case, the mother of a young girl who had cancer pleaded with Manuel to help her daughter. The cancer had progressed so much that there was very little Manuel could do but prescribe some painkillers.

As a result of these experiences, I decided that I wanted to become a doctor. Ultimately, however, Manuel's devotion to his neediest patients, regardless of whether they could pay him, reinforced my passion for sociology and the social sciences, which, thanks to my father, had already been ignited.

Before we left Mexico City, Manuel forcefully suggested that I wear a brace to keep my right foot at a 90-degree angle to my leg to prevent me from tripping so often. Just as he had warned everyone, I blew up and yelled at him, "No, you told me to walk without any help. I am not going to wear a stupid thing like that. I hate all of you!" I stormed out as fast as I could without falling. After months of dutifully following orders, I had finally learned to say "No!" My mother told me that I was not always going to have to wear the brace, and my father added that it would help with walking on the uneven streets in New Orleans. He also added that if anything bad happened to me, Manuel wouldn't be there to help. Realizing that Manuel would not be around to catch me scared the hell out of me and sealed the deal. Manuel drove me to the hospital to get fitted for the brace. I found learning how to walk with the brace awkward as I was not used to walking with my right foot locked in that position. I must admit that it did help reduce my falls, but, with the added weight, it didn't do much to help me lift my right leg high enough to handle the bumpy sidewalks once we returned to New Orleans. That would have to wait until my physical therapy sessions progressed.

A GLOBAL AWAKENING

My family's home base during my early childhood was New Orleans and Tulane University, but we also spent large stints of time in Latin America. The countries and cities we visited throughout Latin America influenced my development much more than my life in Louisiana and the United States. Even in my teens, after we moved to New Hampshire, I continued to experience life outside the United States as I learned French in Vichy, France, with a tour group and later traveled around Europe with my best high school friend Chris.

The insights I gained from each place my family lived in Latin America were influenced not only by my age but also by the different stages of my recuperation. Additionally, it was because these countries were not culturally homogeneous. For example, while many different country's cuisines had the same names for recipes, they differed substantially from one place to another. Similarly, the manner of dress was different in many countries: Argentines wore more plaid clothes while Chileans wore more color-varied clothes.

Beyond these and other cultural differences, the time I had spent with Manuel as he provided lifesaving medical attention to people of all classes eventually led me to think about how the countries diverged socially and politically. While economic development in Mexico increased almost without interruption following its middle-class revolution until the 1960s, the social stratification of the earlier era remained, preventing people from the lower classes from enjoying many of the country's new opportunities. Guatemala was unable to consolidate a smooth political succession process and was never able to initiate a long period of sustained economic growth, although it did have a small but growing middle class interested in promoting economic development and political stability. Chile was enmeshed in a totally different process, both politically and economically, than either Mexico or Guatemala. It had a relatively large middle class and, with three notable exceptions, was accustomed to stable inter-political party dialogue, electoral politics, and presidential successions. The first two exceptions were short-lived interruptions: the first occurred in 1891when President José Manuel Balmaceda was ushering in middle-class entrepreneurship, while the second was in the early 1920s when the country's Constitution was rewritten to reflect the changes in peoples' attitudes from the time of its 1830 Constitution.

* * *

GUATEMALA CITY: AN AFFECTION AND AN AVERSION

The trip my father and I were making to Guatemala when the accident happened was actually a return to that country. My family first lived in Guatemala's capital city in the early 1950s, when my father, with my mother's help, researched the country's process of modernization and its Constitution for his first book, *A Study in Government: Guatemala*. I was three years old at the time, so it was easy to learn any language through imitation. I shifted between English and Spanish as if they were one single language, speaking English to certain people and Spanish to others without much thought.

My father's previous training as a linguist meant he could easily move between languages, using proper grammar and mastering the accents for each country. My mother had a more difficult time using correct Spanish grammar. Tenses tended to trip her up, and, throughout her life, it was only by chance that she used the correct verb tense in Spanish. She often used the past tense when she meant to speak in the present or the future tense when meaning to use the past tense. At other times, her verb tense seemed to be selected at random. I'm not sure why my mother had such trouble using correct tenses. From my short-lived experience teaching English as a second language, it might have stemmed from her efforts to think in English while instantaneously translating her thoughts into Spanish rather than just *thinking* in Spanish. My mother's confusion did not stop people from all economic stations and social backgrounds from understanding her. And she insisted on speaking in Spanish with Latin Americans. I often lapsed into Spanish even when there were both English and Spanish speakers in a group. It usually depended on the person I was looking at when I was talking.

My memories from our first visit to Guatemala City are very scant, but one incident from a weekend trip to the beach sticks out vividly in my mind. We were in the car of our family friend Harvey, a reporter for a U.S. magazine, and his wife Ruth. Harvey was driving, and my father was sitting in the bucket seat next to him. Ruth was in the backseat with her two daughters and my mother had me on her lap. The adults were jabbering about Guatemalan politics, and Harvey and Ruth's daughters Claudia and Carol and I were kvetching because we were bored. My mother told us to count the number of cars we passed along the road. When we got tired of counting every car, we started to keep track of all the gray cars, then all the black cars, and so on.

The adult conversation veered off into a discussion about a rumored coup d'état, which was supposed to be taking place at that very moment. None of the adults were worried, as they thought the conflict would follow the usual pattern set by previous exchanges. The two opposing sides usually presented a list of their supporters and the one with the most would win. Nevertheless, police checkpoints had been set up throughout the country, especially along the Pacific Highway to the ocean, to intercept anyone transporting guns, ammunition, or political pamphlets. Shortly after we left the city's outskirts, we were flagged down at one of these posts. When they saw the officers, both Harvey and my father exclaimed, "Oh, shit!" at the same time. My father immediately regained his composure, turned around, and said, "This will only take a minute." Two young police officers, one on either side of the car, approached and bent down to look at us. The policeman at the driver's window asked, "Are there any guns in the car?"

Harvey answered, "No, there aren't any guns in the car."

The officer wasn't convinced and commanded Harvey, "Get out of the car and open the trunk."

Harvey gave a sigh, got out, and walked to the back of the car. When he opened the trunk, there, in plain sight, were two machine guns and several containers of ammunition. I don't know whether my father and mother were aware that Harvey was carrying weapons.

Although Harvey tried to explain that the guns were to protect his wife, who was the daughter of a diplomat, the officer in charge wasn't swayed in the least. He told Harvey, "Get in your car and follow us to the police station where you will have to explain to the captain the reason that you have these weapons in the car."

One of the officers took the guns and ammunition out of the trunk and put them in the police car. It took about 30 minutes to get to the police station and when we arrived, the officers escorted Harvey and my father into the building while the rest of us were left in the car, entertaining ourselves in the heat. Ruth and my mother moved to the front of the car while Claudia, Carol, and I started to play cards in the back. A policeman bent down, looked through the driver's side window and, noticing that my mother was not a Guatemalan, started speaking English to her. His gaze shifted to the kids in the backseat.

He looked at me, and he asked me in English, "What is your name?"

I replied in Spanish, "My name is Quique." (Quique is the translation of Hank.)

He reverted to Spanish, "Oh, you speak Spanish?"

"Yes."

"Have you ever seen a real gun?" Without waiting for me to say no, he pulled his revolver out of its holster and showed it to me. "Have you ever held a gun?"

"No."

Extending his arm, he said, "Here, take it. You can hold it."

"No, I don't want to." I started looking for a place to hide. I had never felt so frightened in my life, and I think my aversion to guns stems from this incident. I wonder now why anyone would offer a child a loaded gun.

To this day I have no idea what went on there, but eventually, as the clock ticked into the noon hour, Harvey and my father emerged from the police station. Even with this detour, we still had enough time to take a quick swim, have some lunch, and make castles in the sand.

* * *

SANTIAGO, CHILE: PEPI
AND THE CAT

Hank, at our pool in Santiago, Chile

During my father's sabbatical from September 1957 to September 1958, my family lived in Santiago, Chile, and Buenos Aires, Argentina. Although my physical challenges from the accident persisted, it was during this trip that I realized the need to interact and make friends. These efforts brought about both positive and negative results. I attended Nido de Aguilas, Santiago's international school, while my father wrote monthly articles for the American Universities Field Staff and taught a political science class at the Catholic

University and National University. My mother was busy with Benjie and me and assisted my father with his articles.

My parents already had a network of friends and acquaintances from the eight months they had lived in Chile in 1948 for my father's dissertation research. My parents also had another personal connection to Santiago. Even though I was born in Philadelphia, my mother always reminded me, I was "conceived on the banks of the Mapocho River," the city's main river. Scandalous!

At Nido de Aguilas, I became obsessed with arithmetic, no doubt influenced by my mother's bedtime tales of Enrique and Pepi doing their math homework together. I had started long division toward the end of my third-grade year in New Orleans, but I had to learn how to write division longhand in the Latin American style, which is the reverse of the format in the United States (e.g., $45 \underline{|6789} = 150.87$). Luckily, I had Pepi as my invisible partner whenever I did my homework.

I also became interested in chemistry. Well, not so much chemistry as the cat in the sixth-grade chemistry laboratory next-door to our classroom. Whenever we were at recess, my classmates and I watched the beautiful orange tiger cat, perched on top of the teacher's desk, sometimes prancing around the room like she owned it. There were rumors, however, that the school was grooming the cat to be dissected. (It never crossed our minds that it would be more of a biology project than a chemistry experiment.) Our class wrote a petition urging the school to prevent this murder, which everyone in the school signed, and presented it to the principal. She came down to the classroom and explained that it was the teacher's pet cat and that there was no intention to kill it. We were all relieved and elated!

The rector of the Catholic University had given me a dog with a missing right eye as a birthday present. In honor of my imaginary friend, I named him Pepi. I was very protective of Pepi because I felt that we faced similar challenges. Once when I was getting off the school bus, some kids who knew about Pepi's missing eye taunted me about my "retarded" dog. I turned around and yelled at them, "Pepi is a great dog! So, what if he doesn't have a right eye? He's still a great dog!" I was so angry that after I stormed off the bus, I threw my glasses on the ground in rage and frustration. As the bus started to move away, I put up my fists and challenged everyone on the bus to a fistfight. The only downside to this was that my parents had to buy me a pair of new glasses.

In December 1957, soon after the bus incident, my family packed up and boarded an airplane to Buenos Aires. Pepi had a seat all to himself. Tragically, he didn't live long in our new home because he came down with distemper in July 1958. The vet told us that unless they found a cure within a few weeks he would die. I only had only a vague notion about death and couldn't understand why I wouldn't be able to hold, pat, talk to, or walk Pepi anymore. How could the dog that played such an important part in my life be so cruelly taken from me? How could we be separated? How would I be able to do my math homework without Pepi? When he passed, I felt like I had lost my soul mate.

* * *

A RETURN TO SANTIAGO

My connection to Santiago became even deeper when I returned in June 1972 to conduct field research for my Oxford University Bachelor of Philosophy thesis. The country had recently elected Salvador Allende, a member of the Socialist Party and the Popular Unity coalition, as president. I was excited about Allende's victory and curious to find out how the political left had won an election in a capitalist country. What was it about the country's commitment to democratic processes and actions that made it possible for so many citizens to consider the political left legitimate?

Salvador Allende and the Popular Unity coalition, composed of the Socialist, Communist, and Radical Parties and other, smaller, leftist political parties, did not specifically claim that they were going to immediately transform the country into a socialist nation. They did propose during the campaign to set the country on *la via Chilena hace el socialismo* (the Chilean road to socialism). This meant that the 36 percent of Chileans who voted for Allende and the Popular Unity coalition knew the policies they were choosing. Since none of the three presidential candidates received a majority of the popular vote, the parliament had to validate the winner, who usually was the one with the highest vote count. Even though Allende received a plurality of the votes, there was some anxiety among his supporters that he wouldn't be selected as president because almost two-thirds of parliament's legislators were vehemently opposed to him. In the end, however, tradition won, and parliament confirmed Allende as president.

I couldn't believe I was going to experience a peaceful revolution in practice! The travel grant, generously provided by the Latin American Center at Oxford University, was enough to cover my living expenses while in Chile but I had to figure out how I was going to cover my flight to Santiago. As luck would have it, my friend, Larry Burns, who had encouraged me to attend graduate school at Oxford, was writing a travel article for *Lan Chile*, the Chilean Airline. He offered to give me the money he received for writing the article to pay for my flight from Paris to Santiago, since the airline did not have any flights out of England.

At the beginning of June, I took a British Airways flight from London's Gatwick Airport to Paris. I had been in Paris twice before and knew exactly what I wanted to do. After checking into the hotel, I took a cab to the Louvre Museum to revisit some of the exhibits I'd seen as a teenager. I went to a nearby café for a late afternoon snack of a ham and cheese sandwich with a large cup of café au lait, and then walked around the city, ending up at the Luxembourg Gardens. The flight to Santiago the next day was very long. We had several refueling stops, in the Canary Islands, Rio de Janeiro, and Buenos Aires before reaching our final destination. We were not allowed to leave the plane during any of these stops, although some lasted for more than an hour.

Because we had refueled in the Canary Islands, the plane and its passengers had to be fumigated to assure that we did not carry any viruses when we arrived at the Rio de Janeiro airport. Airport staff entered the plane with large canisters of disinfectant, told the passengers to cover and close their eyes, and spayed everything in sight. This was a new experience for me.

Before disembarking in Santiago, I was told by a flight attendant that, because I was a citizen of the United States, I had to exchange $10 into escudos, the Chilean currency, for every day that I would be in Chile. I planned to conduct my research over a three-month period, and the $700 I had would not be enough. I was sure that Joel and Betty Jutkowitz, who were meeting me at the airport, would know how to get around this hurdle, but there was no way to reach them before I had to make the exchange. I decided to say that I would be staying in the country for 60 days and then, if I had to, I'd change some more dollars into escudos. Fortunately, I had a large empty bag with me to carry the 25,200 escudos that I received (the exchange rate was 42 escudos per dollar). After hugs and kisses, I told Joel and Betty about the currency exchange. Joel looked at me incredulously and said, "Schmuck, you should have told them that you were only going to be here for a week, and we would have been able to do something about it." But I had enough money and didn't mind exchanging it. After all, doing so supported the country's initiative to transition to socialism.

As we drove to Joel and Betty's house, which was in a residential section of the city, I was thrilled to see graffiti proclaiming, "*la via Chilena hace el socialismo*," and "*el pueblo unido hamas sera vencido*" (the people united will never be defeated). The reality behind these slogans was precisely what I had come to the country to research and understand. Joel, Betty, and their three children, Eduardo, Monica, and Alex lived in a three-story house with a small patio in the back. Their next-door neighbor had a scaled down amateur zoo inside his house and in the yard around it. I'm not sure whether it was legal, but no one in the neighborhood seemed to mind. One afternoon, a baby bear cub jumped the fence onto our back patio. Everyone in the house was frightened, but I knew no fear. To me, the cub didn't appear to be dangerous, so I went out to the patio and talked to the cub in a very low voice for about 15 minutes. After asking how he was, I told him that he shouldn't have jumped the fence and then gently put him back on the other side. Everybody yelled at me and said that I was lucky the cub's mother wasn't around, but I was very proud of how I handled the situation.

On my first Saturday in Santiago, Joel, Betty, and I drove into the center of the city on Avenida Providencia. At every traffic signal, groups of people stood on the four corners of the intersections handing out brochures and flyers to those who were stopped at red lights. The ideological spectrum was broadly represented, including the Unidad Popular, the centrist Christian

Democratic Party, the politically right National Party, and the far-right Nazi Party. I thought it was fascinating that these various groups were focused on distributing information instead of fighting or yelling at each other. Was the ability to have disagreements in public without violence an element of the democratic action that brought Allende to power?

Not everyone on the sidewalks of Avenida Providencia had politics on their minds. Betty told me that the adolescent and young adult couples strolling together in formal dress were referred to as *los lolos*. I looked at her quizzically, and she explained that in Chilean slang a boyfriend was referred to as a *pololo* and a girlfriend was called a *pola*, and the two were referred to as *los lolos*. The real meaning of a *pololo* is a tadpole worm that slowly winds its way up and down a pole. The word *pololeando* symbolizes the process of the *pololo* and the *pola* winding themselves together in love. If they should become engaged, they would acquire the names *novio* and *novia*.

It was strange to see political activism and courtship taking place side by side, but I soon discovered the calm was only on the surface. Underneath this apparent tranquility was a sinister and turbulent anger toward the Popular Unity's vision for society. This resistance took the form of almost daily demonstrations in the city's business districts. I am not sure how much planning went into these demonstrations, but people representing opposing political views would start to gravitate at either end of a city block. At some undefined time, both groups would, almost simultaneously, start marching toward each other, which cued the police to intervene. Holding their shields in front of their faces with one hand and a baton in the other, they would divide the demonstrators into two groups, then split each smaller group in half, and continue doing this until each demonstrator found him or herself next to a policeman. During this process, there was almost no violence between the police and the demonstrators. After the demonstrators who no longer wanted to participate disbursed, small contingents of each group stayed and continued shouting at one another. At this point, the police would retreat to be replaced by military tanks that rolled forward and sprayed the remaining demonstrators with water. Joel told me that this type of police action was normal during all political administrations.

I happened to be rummaging through a bookstore when one of these spontaneously organized demonstrations occurred. Everyone in the store stared out the window at the protest. The usual ritual repeated itself, the two opposing groups started walking toward each other, the police divided the opposing groups into smaller groups, followed by the departure of those who didn't want to fight further. The difference this time though was that some "opposition" demonstrators poured boiling oil onto the police from the roof of a nearby building. The police responded by shooting tear-gas canisters at them. One of the people throwing the oil was hit by a canister and subsequently died. (After I returned to Norwich that summer, I read about this incident in a national newspaper, however, the person who was killed was reported to have been walking across the street. This is not what I saw, and it was the only demonstration that day.)

The anger of those who could no longer tolerate the Popular Unity's economic and political changes wasn't limited to street demonstrations. Television and newspaper articles correctly pointed out that if the opposition political parties could gain a two-thirds plus one majority in the congress, they could impeach Allende. There were even sinister advertisements calling for the assassination of Allende.

After being in the country for a while, I traced the opposition of the upper and some members of the middle class to the Allende Administration's lowering prices on food items and other staples. Historically, working class Chileans couldn't afford beef on a daily or even a weekly basis, but it was a daily staple for those at higher income levels. Reduced prices made it possible for members of the working class and others with less income to purchase beef, leading to societal as well as nutritional changes that challenged traditional behaviors. For many middle- and upper-income people visiting colleagues after work, there was an unwritten rule that guests who stayed into the dinner hour, usually after nine o'clock, would be asked to stay for dinner, which customarily included a beef course.

Even before the price of beef was lowered, it was a scarce commodity in Chile as there was only a small area of the country, between the desert in the north and the Antarctic and mountainous south, that was good for raising cattle. Therefore, a large part of the country's beef always had to be imported from Argentina or Australia. The cost of foreign beef rose tremendously when the United States began to embargo goods on ships bound for Chile. So, when the government lowered the price of beef, more people could buy it, resulting in a much shorter supply. Families accustomed to a beef course felt a diminished esteem among their friends when they couldn't offer them the standard meat course as part of a meal. Many upper- and middle-class women felt so strongly about this loss that they demonstrated in the streets clanging pots and pans together demanding the overthrow of Allende. Of course, the coalition that elected Allende and Popular Unity contained supporters from these classes. Allende, who was a medical doctor, was a member of the middle class.

Allende's supporters were aware of the division in sentiment that their initiatives were causing and even had a certain sense of humor about it. While I was eating empanadas and drinking pisco sours at a party, a high-ranking member of the Socialist Party said, "I'm going to tell you a joke that in any other country you would think of as treasonous, but it is the situation that we are facing." He continued,

"A Chilean man dies and goes to hell. He knocks on the door of the devil, and when the devil opens the door, he asks, 'What country are you from?'

"The man says, 'I'm from Chile.'

"The devil asks, 'Are you from the UP (the Popular Unity) or a mummy (the political left's name for the opposition)?'

"'I'm apolitical. Why, are there two hells for Chileans?'

"'Yes,' and pointing to the left the devil says, 'There's the hell for the UP,' and pointing to the right, 'There's the mummy's hell.'

"'Can I take a look before I make up my mind?'

"'Sure, go right ahead. I'll be waiting.'

"The man knocks on the mummy's door, and a man who can barely walk opens it and asks, 'What do you want?'

"'How do they treat you here?'

"The man answers with a stammer in his voice, 'They treat us very badly. Every night we are forced to lay down and sleep on a bed of nails; they put a board on top of us and plaster us down with a tractor.'

"'That's terrible! I'm going to check out the UP's hell.'

"He knocks on the UP's door, and a young man opens it and says, 'Welcome compañiero, what can I do for you? How is the revolution in Chile?'

"'I'll tell you, but first tell me how they treat you down here?'

"'Well, they don't treat us too badly. Every night we are forced to lay down and sleep on a bed of nails; they put a board on top of us and plaster us down with a tractor.'

"But, that's the same as the mummy's hell, I'm going over there.'

"'Don't do that compañiero! There are no more nails, the board has disappeared, and there are no spare parts for the tractor.'"

Yes, this was the situation, but the hope (*la esperanza*) was that this condition would improve. Many people in the country believed in Allende's efforts, and the Popular Unity's support was spreading to the traditionally more conservative rural areas of the country. During the March 1973 parliamentary elections, the Popular Unity increased its support from a little more than 36 percent to more than 43 percent. A Christian Democratic Chilean colleague of mine at Oxford told me that this election was the "final straw" and said that it "forced us to form an alliance with the Chilean political establishment" to make plans to overthrow Allende and the Popular Unity because if the coalition were to gain an additional seven percent in the upcoming presidential elections of 1976, they would have a clear mandate to establish a socialist country. My colleague and a number of other Chileans studying at Oxford University disappeared for a week from the university to hatch their plans for a removal of Allende from office.

I completed my research long before the March 1973 elections. I was unable to spend the entire $600 I had exchanged at the airport before I left, even with the many gifts I bought. I gave my remaining escudos to Joel and Betty. On my way back to England, I stopped for a month in Norwich, Vermont, to write a draft of my thesis. Over dinner, I had conversations with my mother and father about the meaning of democracy. We decided that the best way to think of democratic thought and action was as a continuous process to maximize, at all times, individual and collective liberties. My experiences in Chile led me to believe that this only applied to political parties of the left in that country.

Using this understanding of democracy, I argued in my thesis that, throughout their histories, leftist political parties, especially the socialist and communist parties, were always committed to working in coalitions to obtain a high percentage of the popular vote, to work within the legislature to broaden political participation, and to work within the constitutional framework for radical economic and social changes. In fact, the Communist Party had been represented in the Chilean legislature since its founding in 1921 and the Socialist Party since its formation in 1932.

In the conclusion of my thesis, I contrasted the democratic commitment of Chile's left with the anti-democratic nature of other Chilean political parties. I argued that, in Chile, centrist and rightist political parties were not democratic but were only in favor of elections if they could remain at the helm. For example, I remember when a high-ranking member of the Christian Democratic Party and Eduardo Frei's administration came to our apartment on Bleecker Street in New York a month after Allende's election. He took out a piece of paper with a list of names and said, "The people of Chile have sinned, and these Marxists will have to pay with their lives." My father, my mother, and I were aghast, but we did not immediately grasp the full gravity of the statement. We did know that Chile's Christian Democratic Party had its roots in the Phalangist Party of the 1930s and later had a strong corporatist faction. However, we could not fathom that this political party would be the prime mover in the overthrow of a legitimately elected administration.

On September 11, 1973, driven by the urging of the Christian Democratic Party, democracy in Chile came to an abrupt and violent end until the plebiscite, named "*El voto del no,*" in October 1987 that led to new presidential and parliamentary elections. During the period in between these dates, the Chilean government tortured and killed many citizens. The exact number of those killed is still debated, but a low estimate is 3,000 and a high estimate is 100,000. The most famous victim was Victor Jara, who might be called the Pete Seeger of Chile. While Jara was imprisoned in Chile's national football stadium, soldiers forced him to play a Cuatro, a guitar-like instrument, and sing. After each song, the guards chopped off one of his fingers. When he had no more fingers, they made him sing until they cut out his tongue and killed him.

The military violence and murder were not limited to Chile's borders. My father and his colleagues in academia and the Ford Foundation were able to get Orlando Letelier, the Popular Unity's United Nations ambassador, released from a Chilean concentration camp and brought to the United States in 1975. On September 10, 1976, he gave a speech in Madison Square Garden that deemed the military leaders who overthrew Allende's democratically elected administration "traitors." Less than two weeks later, Letelier and his colleague Ronni Moffitt were killed by a car bomb planted by DINA, Chile's National Intelligence Directorate (Pinochet's secret police), that exploded while they were driving around Washington, D.C.'s Sheridan Circle. This assassination was part of a larger pattern of collusion between the Nixon Administration and the Chilean opposition to Allende's Popular Unity administration. Documents released by the State Department in 2015 revealed the Sheridan Circle killings were carried out with Pinochet's knowledge and support.[1]

The violent overthrow of Chile's long tradition of democratic action and its rule for 19 years by anti-democratic factions backed by the financial aid of foreign governments, including the United States, reminded me of *The Ugly American* by Eugene Burdick and William Lederer. My father had urged me to read the novel, which vividly depicts the lack of empathy shown by U.S. diplomats in Southeast Asia just prior to our country's involvement in the Vietnamese civil war, in the early 1960s. The novel consists of a series of vignettes of Burdick and Lederer's work for the foreign service in Southeast Asia during the early to mid-1950s. In a manner eerily similar to the plot of the novel, the tragic, albeit temporary, overthrow of democracy and the loss

---

[1] See John Dinges, "A Bombshell on Pinochet's Guilt, Delivered Too Late," Newsweek, October 14, 2015 (https://www.newsweek.com/2015/10/30/bombshell-pinochets-guilt-delivered-too-late-383121.html).

of life in Chile reinforced Burdick and Lederer's contention that U.S. foreign service representatives remained insufficiently prepared to understand the cultural, social, and political differences between their home nation and the countries where they worked.

* * *

BUENOS AIRES, ARGENTINA: LATE MORNINGS IN PARQUE RIVADAVIA

My family's first sojourn in Buenos Aires was toward the end of 1957. My parents had read up on the city's many hidden treasures, including a city park that reserved every Sunday for stamp and coin collecting and trading. I didn't know that my father was a philatelist before we moved there, but on a Saturday morning shortly after we arrived, he nonchalantly announced that we were going to buy stamp collecting material and were going to Parque Rivadavia to trade and buy stamps the next day.

Not only was I unaware that my father started collecting stamps at an early age, but it was the first time that I had ever heard of the hobby, much less that there were places where people got together to trade and buy stamps! He said, as far as he knew, Buenos Aires was the only city in the world where part of a park was set aside for philately. Unbeknownst to me, before we left New Orleans, my father had packed a bunch of duplicate stamps from his collection. He had added to this collection a number of newly minted Chilean stamps he'd purchased in Santiago.

At the store, he bought an Argentine stamp album and catalogue; stamp tweezers, which had flat ends instead of pointed ones to prevent the stamps from getting nicked; stamp hinges and plastic stamp holders; a magnifying glass; fluid to test for watermarks on the backs of stamps; two packets of unused and cancelled Argentine stamps; a duplicate book; and small clear cellophane envelopes to hold extra stamps.

After unpacking our purchases on the dining room table, my father took out some of the U.S. stamps he brought from New Orleans. We put them into the duplicate stamp book so we would have something to trade the next day in the park. The duplicate stamp book was composed of 13 thin cardboard pages with six rows of clear one-half inch wide celluloid paper running across and attached to each page at the bottom of each celluloid strip and at both ends of each row.

My father told me to be careful not to smudge, wrinkle, or bend any of the stamps because this would decrease their value and make them harder to trade. He demonstrated the best way to handle them, which involved only touching the stamps using the tweezers and never with one's hands. He showed me how to grasp a stamp with the tweezers and carefully slip it between the cardboard and the cellophane strip of the page. At first, this was extremely difficult because the tweezers were in my right hand, but each time I added an additional stamp to the book it became a little easier. I eventually became quite proficient at it. We next put the recently acquired Argentine stamps into our new stamp album. Occasionally, he also checked whether there was a watermark on the back of each stamp because the catalogue value of stamps varies significantly based on the presence and type of watermark. Stamps with a low catalogue value could simply be placed in the album by folding a stamp hinge, licking one side of it and then attaching it to the back side of the stamp, licking the other side of the hinge and then pasting it in its correct place in the stamp album. It was best to place those with higher catalogue values in plastic stamp holders before they were attached to the page in the stamp album. My father said you should never paste the entire back of any stamp to the album page because if you wanted to trade it in the future, this would drastically reduce its value. The process was very meticulous and slow. Not only did I have to decide if a stamp merited a stamp holder, I had to be very precise when placing stamps in the album, and my father encouraged me to concentrate on using my weaker right hand to do so.

Right after breakfast the next day, we started off to Parque Rivadavia. When we arrived at around 9:45, many other stamp collectors were already sitting with their duplicate stamp books waiting for the trading to begin. I was nine years old and appeared to be the youngest person there. The coin collectors were separated from the stamp collectors, but they were in the same general vicinity of the park. There was a tradition that trading could not begin until 10 o'clock sharp. Once the clock struck the hour, people started circulating to see what was available.

This was all new to us, so we sat at our table watching and waiting for other collectors to notice us. Once they figured out that we were foreigners because we weren't dressed like Argentines, they were curious to see what stamps we had. As a trickle of collectors started to head our way, I tensed because I feared that I would not be able to speak the language correctly or say the right thing. After all, this was a new country, whose people spoke an unfamiliar type of Spanish, and I didn't know anyone. Besides, I had hardly spoken with anybody but my family since we arrived in the city. However, my father encouraged me to do all the talking. Some collectors walked away when they saw that all we had to trade were U.S. stamps, though others stayed. While we searched their duplicate books, they looked at ours. Fortunately, we hadn't brought all our U.S. duplicates to the park that day or we probably wouldn't have had any stamps to trade in the future. Within an hour, we had traded everything we brought with us that morning. Before leaving, we headed over to the stamp vendors and bought some additional unused Argentine stamps.

My outings to Parque Rivadavia with my father opened a whole new world for me. I learned how to collaborate and negotiate with others over the value of stamps. I also realized that an entire nation's history could be gleaned from the stamps it produces. Most stamp catalogues not only provide a picture and list the value of each stamp, but also a brief description of their social history. Later in March, when I started school, I often used stamps to supplement the Argentine history that I was learning.

* * *

¡PETITERO!

Through those stamp collecting mornings, I became acquainted with the Spanish spoken in Buenos Aires, which is called Castellano. This dialect was unlike any Spanish I'd heard before. The people spoke with a different rhythm and cadence than in Mexico, where most people spoke with a slightly singing tone, or Chile, where the "s" in words was often swallowed and became silent.

It became evident that certain words had completely different meanings depending on the country. In Argentina, people would not say, "I must catch the next trolley," but rather, "I must take the trolley" because the verb "to catch" signifies in Argentine Spanish "to have sex with someone" in a vulgar way.

I had perfected my newly acquired Castilian accent sufficiently to be completely understood at a grocery store the first time my mother sent me out to buy anchovies. The person at the counter, however, still knew I wasn't a *porteño*, a native of Buenos Aires, probably because of the way I dressed. He asked me where I was from and didn't believe me when I told him I was from the United States. As I was walking back to the apartment from the grocery store, a passerby yelled out to me, "Hey, *petitero*, how are you?" I had no idea what he was talking about, but I figured, correctly as it turned out, that it was a slur. When I returned home, I asked my father what it meant but he didn't know either. After consulting an Argentine dictionary and asking some friends, we concluded that it was a derogatory word used to describe a snobbish, well-dressed, middle-aged, bourgeois family man. In particular, the phrase applied to someone who thought of himself as a highly cultured individual who spoke multiple languages with ease while actually only being able to converse in his native Castellano. While many tangos were written about these people, the word was first coined during the middle years of the 1950s and was out of vogue by 1959. I was curious to know why the passerby had used this word, as I didn't fit the categories in the definition. As we discussed the meaning of this slang over dinner, it became clear that it was an overt conceptualization and acknowledgement of social class distinctions. The force behind this term expressed a viewpoint in stark opposition to my experiences in Mexico. As someone who spoke two languages extremely well, accumulated a bundle of wealth, and climbed several rungs above his origins, Manuel would seem to fit the bill as a *petitero*. However, he was not snobbish in the least and insisted on personally providing services to the poor. He saw himself as a Mexican rather than as a member of a particular social class or exclusive group. This was my overall impression of how Mexicans viewed themselves, although there was a vast gulf between the aspirations, choices, and opportunities of people in different social classes and groups in that country versus in Argentina.

Now that I knew the meaning of *petitero*, I still wanted to better understand the reasons for its use. The answer was actually right in front of me in my stamp collection, the conversations I overheard in the streets, the Argentine history I learned in school, and the intellectual debates my parents had with Argentine colleagues. It was a shorthand stereotype that painted a vivid picture of a society undergoing a wrenchingly rapid political and economic transformation, a society that was attempting to implement a process of industrialization.

Argentina was changing quickly, and the transition brought out people's anxieties. Many of their fears were related to the coup in September 1955 that removed the country's strongman leader Juan Peron, the interim presidential administration of Pedro Eugenio Aramburu, and the subsequent presidential election of Arturo Frondizi in February 1958. A few years later, in school I learned that President Peron's major accomplishment was his effort to increase the country's economic and social well-being by forming an alliance between its rural and urban populations, something no one had successfully achieved before. The trick to sustain this alliance appeared to primarily rest on a thriving economy and the charisma of his wife, Eva. When Eva died in 1952 and the economy started to collapse, this alliance rapidly fell apart and Peron's presidency began to unravel.

Arturo Frondizi, the winning candidate in the February 1958 elections, could have easily been labeled a *petitero* because of his strong emphasis on and support for rapid urban development at the expense of rural agricultural production, increasing direct foreign investment to fortify heavy industry, strengthening sagging auto and energy extraction industries, and promoting better and faster infrastructural development. One of the slogans chanted by supporters of Frondizi's opponent Ricardo Balbin that could be heard in the streets was, "Squash, vegetables, Frondizi to the garbage" (*Zapallos, verduras, Frondizi a la basura*), which negatively referenced Frondizi's emphasis on urban growth to the neglect of rural areas. Yet, on May 1, Frondizi was elected president.

SADDLING UP

When I was almost twelve years old, my family had our 1960 summer vacation in Piriapolis, a small resort town on the banks of the Rio de la Plata in Uruguay. This holiday was notable for two reasons. One was that I read a book in its entirety for the first time. Reading was always challenging because of the effects of the accident. I could still only read with one eye, which didn't move from side to side, so I had to move my head to go from word to word on the page. None of these difficulties, however, were going to stop me from becoming an avid reader. The book was a biography of Julius Caesar, and I imagined that I was in ancient Rome standing in front of the Roman Forum with my arms stretched out wide, proclaiming, "I came, I saw, I conquered!" (As I'll discuss later, I fulfilled this dream when I visited Rome as a teenager.) The second reason was my obsession with learning to ride horses, which stemmed from my passion for *Gunsmoke*, *Bonanza*, and other television Westerns. Despite their protests, I eventually convinced my parents to let me take riding lessons. They agreed on the condition that my mother took riding lessons with me.

Our instructor was an 82-year-old man who had won a medal in dressage at the 1936 German Olympics. Shortly after winning, he was forced to flee Germany because the Nazis discovered that he was Jewish. He had not mounted a horse in nearly 20 years, and, except for our last lesson, didn't get in the saddle while teaching us. He taught us in a secluded area of town crisscrossed with gravel roads and blocks and blocks of trees and bushes but no houses. We had lessons twice a week with the same horses. My horse Chiquita ("Little") was huge, and Grande, my mother's horse, was even larger. I always brought the horses an apple and a carrot for the beginning of each session. Sometimes, they didn't even wait for me to give them their treats but instead went straight for the treats, which I kept in my pocket.

My mother and the instructor had to help me onto Chiquita each time, as I still didn't have the leg strength to manage without assistance. Once I was on the horse, I had good form. During the first few lessons, we learned the basics of letting the horse know when we wanted to go forward, turn left or right, or stop. Then we spent time learning how to trot. Finally, the teacher said that he was going to show my mother how to gallop but wasn't going to teach me because I couldn't grasp the horse tightly enough with my right leg. His decision didn't sit well with me but there was nothing I could say or do to change his mind. Not to be outdone by my mother, I went around a corner while she was busy with the instructor and gently tapped Chiquita on her rear with the whip. After she started to trot, I said in a loud voice, "Galope, Chiquita!" and gave her another little tap on her back with the whip. To my surprise, she started galloping and, to my delight, I felt like I was gliding through the air. When I pulled back on the reins just a little, she slowed to a trot and then to a fast walk. When I rejoined the teacher and my mother, they somehow knew exactly what I had been up to and took turns telling me to be careful if I did it again. But there was no stopping me.

As a graduation present, the teacher mounted a horse and the three of us rode on a completely new and hilly, steep path for our final lesson. I had never been on a trail like this before, and the instructor told me I shouldn't gallop downhill because it was difficult to keep a steady balance. However, I nudged the horse to start galloping and did not see the downhill slope ahead until it was too late to slow Chiquita. My right foot came out of the stirrup and I started to fall off the horse. All I could do was grab the horse's mane and hold on for dear life. Chiquita eventually slowed to a stop and knelt so that I could roll off.

The teacher and my mother watched petrified, but physically speaking, I was not hurt at all. I was furious because they saw me goof up during my last lesson, but also because I didn't want anyone to see my flaws. After the car accident, I always did my best to hide my obvious physical difficulties with activities other people seemed to have no trouble doing. I convinced both my mother and teacher that I wasn't hurt, and they helped me re-mount Chiquita, and I had my last gallop of the summer. I gave both horses an extra final treat before we went home.

ARGENTINA OTRA VEZ

At the end of my father's sabbatical, we briefly returned to New Orleans. Because of my parents' objections to the New Orleans City Council's negative reaction to the two *Brown vs. Board of Education* decisions, my father started looking for another teaching position as soon as we were back in the United States. He also applied for and received a grant from the United Nations to examine the meaning and role of education in Argentina, Chile, Brazil, and Mexico. To do this, he decided that it would be best to be based in Buenos Aires.

I was really excited about the trip to Buenos Aires since this time we were going to travel by ocean liner, and I had never been on a ship before. We would depart from New York City and arrive in Buenos Aires 22 days later, after brief stops in Rio de Janeiro and Sao Paulo. Shortly after the academic school year ended in June 1959, we left New Orleans in our station wagon, which we were also taking to Buenos Aires. When we finally arrived there, the Rosenbergs—Bernard, Sarah, and their daughter Dinah—met us at the dock. Bernard was a sociologist on sabbatical who was conducting research and teaching at several universities in city. He and his family had been in Buenos Aires for six months and were planning to stay for six more. They drove us to 1790 Guise, the three-story house my parents had rented before leaving New Orleans. We would be staying in Palermo, a largely residential neighborhood close to the city center and only 20 blocks from where we had lived the first time.

We had never met the Rosenbergs before, so we introduced ourselves during the car ride. Dinah, who was my junior by two years, immediately informed me, "I am fluent in Yiddish, Hebrew, and Castellano in addition to English so let me do the talking." She turned to her mother for approval and asked, "Isn't that so, mommy?" I never got the chance to tell her that I had learned Castellano, the *porteño* Spanish, during my first visit to Buenos Aires. But I was impressed and somewhat jealous that she spoke so many languages.

A week later, I found out that her linguistic talents were limited when our mothers took us out to lunch. A typical Argentine lunch consisted of several courses, including an empanada appetizer, short ribs with mashed potatoes and a green vegetable as the main course, a salad, flan for dessert, and, to top it all off, a cup of coffee-milk—half-coffee/half-boiled milk. As our lunch loped along at a leisurely pace, it seemed like the meal would never end. I could hardly stay awake and became extremely cranky, so our mothers suggested that Dinah and I take a taxi to the nearby Parque San Martin. Once in the taxi, Dinah told the driver where we wanted to go, but her accent was so terrible that the driver couldn't understand her. After repeating the destination several times, he still didn't get what she was trying to say. I started laughing uncontrollably, at which point, Dinah turned to me angrily and yelled, "If you can tell him where we want to go, tell him or shut up." I then told the driver where we were headed, and we were on our way. Dinah was furious, and I realized that I shouldn't have laughed, but she did say that she could speak Spanish fluently, though had neglected to mention her accent.

* * *

MAKING FRIENDS

Anyone taking a quick look at the facade of our house on 1790 Guise would see a two-story house, but there was also a third floor at the back of the house, which was only accessible from a staircase on the second floor. The double window on the first floor had a short windowsill with a railing where people would normally place flowers or plants, but I used it to sit and daydream. One day while sitting there, four boys from the neighborhood started walking around our car and exclaiming how nice it looked. They praised its red and white paint job, its fins, its dashboard, and the bicycles inside. Although I was twelve years old, I was too bashful to say anything and tried to hide behind some curtains so they wouldn't notice me—but they did. One of the boys came over and asked, "Is that your family's car?"

"Yes."

"Where are you from?"

I pointed toward the sky because all our maps had the north at the top of the page.

"You're from the sky! You're from *heaven*?" he asked.

"No, I am from America."

"But Argentina is in America. We are American, and you are not Argentine."

"No, I'm from the north," I responded.

"Oh, you're from Mendoza," he said.

"No, I'm from the United States," I stated.

"We are the United States of Argentina."

"No, I'm from New York," I said, although, aside from boarding the ocean liner there, I had never really been to New York.

"Ah," he said, "the United States of America! Welcome to Buenos Aires, my friend."

He said his name was Hector Arias and introduced me to the rest of the kids. As I mentioned earlier, this exchange taught me the importance of precise descriptions and to never to assume your country of birth is the center of the universe.

The five of us became close friends and often rode our bikes through the city together. We played *futbol* on the sidewalk in front of our houses. It was the first time that my physical challenges—for example, after kicking the ball I often fell—didn't make me uncomfortable, because though they had to have noticed, they didn't say anything. During the Christmas holidays, we put firecrackers into the hollowed-out pockets of the wall next to our house, lit them, and watched the ants and roaches scatter out after they exploded.

Our return to Buenos Aires also meant I could resume my visits to Parque Rivadavia to build my rapidly growing stamp collection. Now that I was older, I went without my father. I became a regular trader and quite adept at instantaneously assessing the condition and value of a stamp without having to look up the stamp in the catalogue. I also had a better understanding of which stamps I was missing, and as a result was able to more rapidly assess the stamps I needed in a trade. I began to meet some kids my own age during these mornings, and we often went to a restaurant after the trading ended. Even at a very young age, it was common for kids to go out by themselves in Buenos Aires. The owners and employees were always welcoming and offered us free treats like an extra dessert or soda. When we didn't want to have lunch, we went to a café and simply had a coffee-milk with a sweet bun.

* * *

AN EX-PAT EDUCATION

Once my Sundays in the park were over, it was time for another school week to begin. I had to travel almost 25 miles to the Lincoln School in the suburb of La Lucila, where most U.S. expatriates and diplomats lived. Living in La Lucila or its nearby surroundings made it easy for the other students to study and socialize with each other. Whenever I wanted to hang out with them, my father or mother had to drive me to their homes and then drive back to pick me up.

Every school day started with the students in each grade standing together at attention in double rows on the playground facing the flags of the United States of America and Argentina that hung on either side of the school's entrance. With our right hands covering our hearts, we would recite the Pledge of Allegiance and sing the Argentine National Anthem. The school day was also divided between classes taught in English in the morning and Spanish in the afternoon.

Although I had each subject twice a day, the content differed in the English and Spanish sessions. The material covered in the history, social science, and mathematics classes taught in Spanish seemed more advanced than what the English classes covered. During the English sessions, we concentrated primarily on the history, politics, society, and culture of the United States, with world affairs occasionally sprinkled into the mix. During the Spanish sessions, the focus was almost exclusively on Argentine issues but would, at least tangentially, bring up other Latin American issues.

While these differences were probably a reflection of a need to conform to the educational standards of both countries, the school's curriculum presented a personal and immediate issue for me. While I had become extremely well versed in speaking and thinking, not to mention dreaming, in Spanish after the accident, I hadn't truly mastered reading or writing in English. When I spoke or read English, I found it difficult to capture and understand the contextual meaning of a word rather than its more literal dictionary definition. During one test on medieval history, an essay prompt asked for a description of a feudal peasant, and I proudly included in my answer the fact that all feudal peasants were bachelors. That night, my mother received a call from my bewildered teacher, who could not fathom where I could have gotten this idea. My mother didn't know either, so after getting off the phone, she asked me about my reference. With certainty, I replied, "Because in the book it says that peasants are married to the soil, so how can they be married to people?" I took out the textbook and opened it to the page where I'd read this. My mother chuckled and explained that the actual way a word is understood often changes when it is used in different contexts. She called the teacher back and explained my reasoning, although, unfortunately, it didn't raise my grade on the test.

* * *

BUS ADVENTURES

Since I had different school schedules from my friends in the neighborhood, I didn't have any time to hang out with them. It was also hard to make friends with my classmates because I lived so far away from most of them. Obviously, it would have been better to live closer to school, but my parents needed to live close to their academic colleagues. In an effort to resolve my social dilemma, my parents hatched a scheme that allowed me to take public transportation home after my morning classes. The only downside was that I missed the afternoon Spanish classes, but when it came to a decision between friends and classes, I gladly gave up the classes. My parents were able to obtain a note from the family doctor that said spending an entire day at school was creating physical problems for me.

They then had to find a way for me to navigate the public transportation system since there was no school bus to take me home in the middle of the day. They found that if I took the Number 229 bus, I could get off just two blocks from our house and walk the rest of the way home. The bus started its route 15 blocks away from the school, which was much too far for me to walk, but they then discovered that I could take a Number 35 bus, which stopped only a block away from school and could let me off right in front of where the 229 started its route. Once I was on the 229 bus, they figured that it would take close to an hour for me to get home because of traffic and the number of stops the bus had to make. It was a learning experience for me. The longer I took the 229 bus, the more I realized that there was a bus culture reserved only for the bus drivers and the regular riders. Once I became a regular rider, I was slowly included in this culture. Regular riders had their specified seats and, if someone occupied someone else's seat, he or she would get up and move. The regulars would chat amongst themselves. I sat on the right side of the bus, which had a row of single seats, across and diagonally behind the driver and behind the right front door of the bus. It was the only exit and entry except for the emergency exit that, luckily, we never had to use. Often, but not always, the bus driver had to help me onto the bus because of its high steps. It was funny when new riders broke bus norms. Once, three Catholic nuns got on the bus a few bus stops after the start of its route. There were only two empty seats available so one of the nuns turned to me and commanded, "Give your seat to God!"

I responded, "No!" Although Argentina was largely a Catholic country, out of the corner of my eye I could see the bus driver and the others silently chuckle while the nuns told me how disgraceful and sacrilegious, I was. I stayed in my seat, and nobody on the bus except the nuns seemed to care.

Every day I exited the bus a block away from 1790 Guise and walked past a building with two guards stationed outside wearing armbands and holding a strange flag. After walking by the building a few times, I became curious and asked my mother why they were standing there, what their arm insignias meant, and the purpose of the building. She told me that it was the Nazi Party Headquarters, and the insignia was a swastika. Over the course of the next few weeks, she told me about Hitler, the Holocaust, and the atrocities of World War II. In history class, we had not yet started learning about the 20th century. She told me that while there was a large Argentine Jewish community, there was also a large German community, many members of which were ex-Nazis who had sought political asylum in the country at the end of the war. From that day forward, and, until we left Buenos Aires, I never walked on the same side of the street as that building again. We always talked politics at home, but this was all new to me. My parents told me that, as World War II ended, many German Jews as well as members of the German Nazi Party sought asylum in Argentina as well as other countries in Latin America and that it was customary to admit those seeking asylum.

* * *

AN ACCIDENT

Instead of having a Bar Mitzvah for my 13th birthday in 1961, my mother took me horseback riding. I was riding in front of my mother when I heard her horse make a strange sound. I turned around in time to see her horse run past me without my mother, who was lying flat on the ground. Something had frightened the horse, and it had reared up and thrown my mother off. By the time I reached her, a crowd had gathered. It was obvious she was in excruciating pain. Someone said that they'd already called for an ambulance from a nearby phone kiosk. He then asked for my father's name and our home telephone number, and once I gave him the information, he ran off to call my father. I kept pleading with my mother not to close her eyes because, in my mind, if she did, she would die. I started telling her jokes or anything I could think of to keep her awake. Whenever I saw that she was about to nod off, I would give her a little shove. The ambulance arrived quickly, so I did not have to keep this up for very long.

After she was on a stretcher and given a painkiller, the paramedics put my mother into the ambulance. She had broken a vertebra in her lower back and had to stay in the hospital for two weeks. When she was released, she had to wear a cast from her shoulders to just above her pelvic area with a large circle cut out of it around her belly button so that some air could circulate under the cast. She was told to stay in bed for another two weeks and then, after a follow-up evaluation, she would be able to start slowly and briefly walking around the house.

* * *

LOST AND FOUND IN MUSIC

Parque Rivadavia's Sunday morning stamp and coin trading venue was only one of the cultural wonders of Buenos Aires. The city is also known as the tango capital of the world and has many classical music and opera venues. I regularly attended classical concerts with my parents. The most memorable of these was listening to Beethoven's *Ninth Symphony* in the extremely elegant and prestigious Teatro de Colón Theater in Buenos Aires, which sat up to 2,500 people among its many concert and opera halls. Before the concert began, my mother told me, as she did at every concert, to keep my mouth open a little because when I breathed only through my nose, I'd make sniffling sounds, which would annoy the people sitting around us. I kept my mouth slightly open but whenever I forgot, my mother nudged me.

The music was intoxicating! I could not get over the strength and assertiveness of the piece or the gusto with which the orchestra played the symphony, and not just in its grand finale, the *Ode to Joy*. After listening to the symphony, I decided I wanted to start playing an instrument again. I had a sneaking feeling this was the main reason my parents took me to these concerts. The only question was which instrument would allow me to focus on the music rather than my physical challenges. After some discussion on our way home, we decided that the piano would be best. I could take lessons and would be able to practice while sitting down, something not encouraged for a number of other instruments. And, we already had a piano, which only needed tuning, at the house at 1790 Guise.

An Argentine family friend put us in touch with a concert pianist to help us find a good teacher, but instead he decided to teach me himself. At my first lesson, my mother explained that it would be difficult for me to use the right piano pedal as my right leg and foot were rather weak. My instructor taught me a new scale every week and insisted that I always focus some attention on the Hanon *Etudes* when I practiced. I particularly liked Carl Orff's beginner piano book, and I later learned pieces composed by Beethoven, Mozart, Bach, and Clementi. Whenever I played the piano, my mind drifted into tranquility where nothing mattered but the sweet sounds of the notes.

* * *

MEXICO CITY'S TWO SIDES: TAKE ME FOR A RIDE IN YOUR CAR, CAR

After the second time we lived in Buenos Aires, we moved to Hanover, New Hampshire, where my father was given a full professor's position in the Political Science Department and my mother a position as an instructor in the Sociology Department at Dartmouth College. Because I found it hard to assimilate to small town life, my parents thought it would be fun for me to get away for a while. They asked Manuel and Beulah if I could visit them for the month of June. I was excited when my parents told me where I would be going. Not only because I would be returning to my old haunts in Mexico City or that I would be seeing Manuel and Beulah, but, at the age of 14, it would be my first unaccompanied flight. Though I wasn't especially nervous or scared I was somewhat concerned that things might go awry or something bad might happen. As it turned out, changing planes at LaGuardia Airport was quite easy, and I didn't need any assistance getting from one plane to the next. Manuel and Beulah were waiting at the airport when I arrived in Mexico City, and they quickly drove me to their house. I had never been to their home before and was amazed at its humongous size. It had three floors that were parallel to the three levels of the backyard, which descended and overlooked a valley. On the lowest level, there was a cave built into the side of the mountain where they stored wine and liquor, and also had a bar with a jukebox. I often went into the cave and pretended that I was Pancho Villa hiding from U.S. soldiers who were looking to arrest or kill me because of my incursions into Texas.

Mexico City is famous for motorists who drive their cars with abandon, hardly ever stopping for red lights, and weaving from one lane to the other without regard for other cars on the road. It was in this environment that I learned how to drive. One Saturday afternoon, Manuel came down for lunch dressed in his Army uniform and announced, quite nonchalantly, that I was going to drive his gray, 1940-ish Ford, which had to be started with a choke, into the center of the city. Even though I was only 14 years old and had never driven before, I wasn't going to pass up this chance! As soon as he settled into the passenger seat, Manuel started to explain how to drive correctly. He told me that the right foot, which was my bad one, was supposed to be used for the choke, gas pedal, and the brake. He also cautioned that I should never use my left foot for these actions because I might forget which foot to use in an emergency and have a deadly accident. The left foot was essentially supposed to rest on its side on the car's floor, except when it was needed to press the clutch down to change from one gear to another. I needed to release the clutch immediately after the gears shifted or the car would lurch forward. First though, I needed to turn the key and pump the choke several times with my right foot to start the car. This was of course difficult for me because of the limited strength in my leg, but after numerous tries I succeeded. After making sure that nobody was walking behind the car and there were no cars coming down the street, I slowly backed out of the driveway.

As we drove along El Paseo de la Reforma toward the city center, Manuel instructed me on what I should do and what to pay attention to while driving. He told me that the easiest way to make sure I stayed in my lane was to visually line up the hood ornament with the right-hand lane markers on the street. This would ensure that I was in the center of the lane in which I was driving. He also said it was important to be aware not only of what was on the road ahead but to check the rearview mirrors for what was behind and on both sides of me. While Manuel talked, I drove through crowded streets and slowly figured out how to compensate for my inability to focus both eyes at the same time. I drove with my left eye looking forward, to the sides and, using the rearview mirror on the driver's door, to the left rear. Because

I could not move my right eyeball from the corner of its socket, my right eye was almost constantly focused on the front window's rearview mirror. This way I could always see the traffic behind me. I became aware that while I saw different things with each eye, they worked in concert with each other. When something was too far to the right for my left eye to view it, my right eye took over. I discovered I was "unconsciously conscious" of what each eye was doing all the time. I never saw double, and never thought that the traffic ahead of us was the traffic behind, or vice versa. When I needed to shift eyes, I just did so automatically.

I was having the time of my life until Manuel suggested we make a circle at an upcoming roundabout and head home. I missed a stoplight while going around the circle, and the next thing I heard was a police motorcycle siren. I pulled over to the side of the road and waited for the policeman to come to the car's window. He asked to see my license and the car's registration. Manuel took the registration out of the glove compartment, which I gave to the policeman. I then told him, "I don't have a license."

He looked at me quizzically and said, "Well then, I will have to take both of you to the police station."

I responded, "Why don't you tell that to my uncle, General Sanchez-Garibay."

As the policeman looked toward Manuel, wearing his Army uniform with three stars on both of its shoulders, his face went pale. He instantaneously put his hand to his forehead in a salute. "Excuse me, my general! I did not see you. I am sorry to have stopped you and your nephew. Please say hello to your wife for me, and please don't say anything bad about me to my chief." Looking at me, he said, "Be very careful to stop at every stoplight." I then realized why Manuel had worn his uniform.

When I returned home to Hanover, I told my family about our driving adventure and my discovery that I could instinctively switch back and forth from looking ahead with my left eye and looking at the rearview dashboard mirror with my right eye. In the end, the trip to Mexico was a well-executed plan, hatched by Manuel and my parents, to test my abilities to navigate under new and stressful situations. That those conditions included driving a car with a choke into the maze of Mexico City proved empowering. As for negotiating with a policeman about a missed stoplight, well that too was a challenge I passed with flying colors!

* * *

THE COLEGIO DE MEXICO

I didn't return to Mexico City until September 1975, when I started a year's work as a visiting professor teaching a class on the Comparative Politics of Latin America at The Colegio de Mexico. I also started to conduct research on perceptions of nationalism among different social and economic strata of Mexican society. I was thrilled to return; however, my perceptions of Mexican society had changed dramatically from when I'd previously visited Manuel. Older and wiser, my viewpoints were focused on studying the contrast between the extremes of wealth and poverty and negative analyses about the extent of democracy in Mexico.

When I first arrived, I stayed with Manuel and Beulah, but soon moved within walking distance of work. While living with them, I either caught a public bus or a *pesero* to work, since their home was quite a distance from the Colegio. (A *pesero* is a shared taxi that only costs a few pesos and travels a set route. The *pesero* I took went along the Paseo de la Reforma.) The other riders were an assortment of people from different income levels and occupations. My favorite activity was to start conversations with the other passengers and the driver about their thoughts on the current economic and political conditions in Mexico. The nearly unanimous response was usually that things were worse than before. When I asked what they meant by "before," there were varied responses—some discussed the student strikes in the early 1970s or the massacre of 1968, while some went back much further, referencing the country's middle-class revolution between 1910 and 1917.

I also enjoyed listening to the different accents and would often silently imitate them in order to learn to pronounce some native Mexican words. For example, I had a problem pronouncing *Chapultepec*, a famous castle and park in the city named for the chief of the native Mexicans before the Spaniards invaded the country. One morning on a city bus, I was standing behind a woman with her daughter in her arms as she repeated the word Chapultepec for the toddler over and over again. She separated the word syllable by syllable, narrowing the silence between each syllable just a little, and then she'd speed up the cadence each time she said the full word. By the time I got off the bus, we were both saying the word at just the right pace and accentuation. I still use this technique when I have trouble properly pronouncing a word.

Shortly after I started teaching, I had lunch with a Mexican political science professor who was tenured at the Mexican Autonomous University and three students I'd met at the University of Oxford. The professor had written a convincing book criticizing his country's commitment to democratic processes, so I naturally figured that he'd eventually talk about this critique. I especially hoped that he would comment on the disparities between what was in the media and other literature, and what I heard from many including those I spoke with on the pesero, that conditions, whether economic, political, or social, had not improved much, if at all, in quite some time.

After our greetings, I launched into this discussion, commenting that, "People I've spoken to say that in many ways the political and economic situation in Mexico is worse now that it has ever been."

He replied, "Who have you spoken to?"

I said, "Every day I take a *pesero*, and I usually start a conversation by asking the driver and the other passengers what they think of the political and economic conditions of the country."

He said, "Yeah, well, you asked the wrong people."

And that was all he said on the subject. We continued talking about our work and the best places to go sightseeing.

I was slightly confounded by the difference between how free the professor's critique of the country was in his book and when he was abroad, teaching at Oxford, and his unflinching personal defense of it now that he was back in Mexico. Why would he write such a scathing book on democracy in Mexico and verbally defend the very thing that he was criticizing? The book pointed to the extreme poverty and the lack of educational opportunities for many in the country. Yet the early twentieth century Mexican Revolution had permitted many of the middle class to vastly increase their educational and occupational opportunities as well as their income and wealth. And while some, such as Manuel, were able to overcome the confines of their social class standings, this professor was not able to do so.

The Colegio's administration assured me that I could teach my class in English as all the students understood and spoke English quite well, but I told them I'd prefer to conduct the class in Spanish. The students were all from well-to-do families and had gone to very prestigious secondary schools. They all claimed to be familiar with Mexican politics, and many were involved in some form of political activity, whether as members of a counterculture poetry cooperative or working with a political party. They were too young to have taken part in the student/worker strikes of the late 1960s and early 1970s. The student/worker coalition of 1968 was created in response to the rapid growth of Mexico's GDP at the same time that visible labor abuses and extreme income inequalities became increasingly apparent throughout the country. It was during a march of this coalition that government snipers fired on protestors in what became known as the Tlatelolco massacre.

I was fascinated by the students' insistence that, since they were Latin Americans, they understood the political, social, and economic conditions in *all* of the Latin America countries, even without having read a book or an article on them. They found it difficult to fathom how I, being from the United States, could understand anything about the region's politics, economics, or culture. Therefore, I decided to let the discussions of the class texts they read, almost all of which were written by Latin Americans, guide the class dialogue, and then to add my insights to the conversation. Indeed, many started questioning both the authenticity of what they'd read and their own preconceived notions about people living in other Latin American countries.

I was interested in empowering students to form their own opinions about what they read, saw, and experienced, and then elaborate on my understanding of Mexican politics. I found their reaction to one situation very telling. There was an upcoming election in a state south of Mexico City, and the polls indicated that one of the opposition parties, the Popular Socialist Party (PPS), was going to win about 70 percent of the vote while the other opposition party, the National Action Party (PAN), was going to get 20 percent of the vote. To avoid this, the Institutional Revolutionary Party (PRI), which had only lost a few elections since its founding in the early 1930s, moved all the voting booths and did not let anyone know their new locations. It also put many opposition leaders in jail. The PPS, nevertheless, won the election. In the end, the PRI did not allow any of the winners to take their seats: instead, they installed their own candidates as winners. This provided for a very lively town hall-type class session with some of the students agreeing with the PRI's action, others shrugging their shoulders and proclaiming that this is just the way things are done in Mexico, and the remainder saying that PPS candidates should have been allowed to assume their roles. When I pointed out that in a system committed to tranquil leadership succession that this would not occur, they, unanimously, proclaimed Mexico not to have a democratic tradition.

* * *

EUROPE: VICHY

My Classmates in Vichy

My first trip to France was to take an intensive French language course during the summer after my sophomore year of high school in Hanover. Both Micheline Lyons, who was from France and taught French, and her husband Gene, who taught political science at Dartmouth College, highly recommended Arista Tours to my parents. Their program featured a two-day stay in Paris at the beginning of a seven-week stay in Vichy, one day in Geneva, and one night back in Paris before departing. In Vichy, we were going to speak, read, and write only French. The tour group embarked from New York on a five-day ship voyage to Le Havre followed by a short train ride to Paris.

The architecture in Paris and the Parisian mannerisms were very similar to those in Buenos Aires, so I felt right at home, which helped make it easier for me to acculturate and think (and dream!) in French. We toured Paris by bus, stopping at attractions like the Luxembourg Gardens and the Sorbonne. I loved walking through the Louvre Museum and was awestruck by the number of paintings on display and the extraordinary size of its rooms. I paid particular attention to Jacques-Louis David's *Coronation of Napoleon*. Our guide said that the next day we would see an exact replica of the painting at the Versailles Palace, also painted by David, except that Napoleon's cape had been painted in a different color.

I was usually left alone to fend for myself the entire time we were in Vichy. While I was two or three years younger than everyone else in the group, my forced isolation could have been a result of my odd way of walking and other physical challenges. Whatever the reason, I did a lot on my own, including attending a number of concerts and operas. In fact, I went to Mozart's *The Marriage of Figaro* and Beethoven's *Violin Concerto* twice because I liked them so much. During the intermission of the second performance of the *Violin Concerto*, I had my first conversation in French with a girl who was my age. It went quite well considering that all of my interactions in French until that point had been with adults who spoke English and would let me know if I said something incorrectly.

I felt so free I began to tell her things that I normally kept to myself. "You know," I said, "from the very start of this piece, I started dreaming that I was the soloist and was standing up there on stage for the world to hear me play this beautiful music."

She giggled and asked, "Do you play the violin?"

I replied, "No, I used to play the violin a little but started taking piano lessons in Buenos Aires and am continuing to take lessons in Norwich. I don't play very well."

She said, "Now I understand. I take piano lessons, too, and would also love to be on stage performing."

After the concert, her parents invited me to join them at a nearby café where we continued talking. Unfortunately, they were returning home to Paris the next morning, but Marie-Claire gave me her address and said that if I was ever in the city, I should look her up.

I also met people in Vichy's Parc des Sources, the city's main park, where people sat on benches drinking the city's medicinal mineral water: the city's claim to fame (other than its sordid political past during World War II). Vichy Water, containing sodium bicarbonates and other alkaline salts, is supposed to have curative powers. I tried some, and I can attest to its powers, as I was confined to my bathroom for nearly six hours!

Whenever I sat in one of the parks, someone would inevitably sit down next to me and ask where I was from and what I was doing in town. I'd say that I lived in a small town in Vermont that was much smaller than Vichy and about 400 kilometers north of New York City. These conversations usually went in a number of directions, but they all came back to the same question, "Why are you in Vietnam?" However, their country's failures in Vietnam never seemed to come up as they raged over the U.S. involvement there. I found this question to be perplexing as it felt like I was being equated with the actions of my country's government, actions that I thoroughly detested. While I certainly associated Hitler with Germany, I didn't associate each individual German with all of Hitler's evils. No matter how many times I was asked this question, the reasons behind it remained a puzzle.

Some evenings, I went to a discotheque to dance (as best I could) and meet people. In between dances, I talked to people about politics in France. Whenever they discovered where I was from, they would always turn the conversation toward the shortcomings of the United States. After a few of these interactions, I noticed something interesting. Most opened with a tirade against the U.S. military involvement in Southeast Asia, before expressing their admiration for the opportunities the United States affords its population. When I pointed out significant domestic injustices in the United States, nearly everyone thought that the United States offered unlimited affluence and opportunity for almost all of its citizens. It was hard to know if the sentiments of the people I encountered truly reflected French attitudes in general, as Vichy was only one small slice of the country and very much a university town.

Another odd question that came up quite regularly was, "Who killed John Kennedy?" This was never on the top of my mind, and I had no opinion, but the French were very persistent and had many theories. Was the assassination part of a Soviet plot? Was it a Cuban operation? Was it a right-wing plot by American citizens? Was it instigated by the Central Intelligence Agency? Did Lyndon Johnson orchestrate it? I wondered why this was so important to them. Clearly, part of their fascination with the assassination was the juxtaposition between Kennedy's liberal domestic policies and his hawkish foreign agenda, but there could definitely be other answers as well.

I became such a fixture at the discotheque that before I left Vichy, the maître d' asked me to send him a Kennedy half-dollar when I returned to the United States. We encountered choppy waters on our travels back to the United States, but I found a genial spot in the middle of the ship where it did not rock excessively. As luck would have it, this was also where people were playing poker. I stayed in the game for almost the entire five-day trip, playing poker nonstop, except with short breaks for meals and sleep, and won $500.

* * *

NEW HORIZONS

After my experiences in Vichy, I was itching to revisit the museums of Paris and see more of Europe. The year following my Vichy adventures, Chris, my best high school friend, and I decided that we wanted to travel around Europe for a month between our Junior and Senior high school years. It just so happened that Chris' father was scheduled to go to a conference in Budapest in August. The entire family was planning to travel around Europe for a month before the conference. Both of our families worked it out so that Chris and

I could go off on our own. We would stay with his family in Paris for a few days and then meet up with the rest of the family in Vienna to travel with them to Budapest.

Chris and I used a $150-month Eurorail train pass that allowed us travel anywhere in Europe we wanted to go. We also bought a European travel guidebook, which gave tips about traveling through Europe on $5 a day and recommendations for the best hostels to spend the night. We planned to start our journey in London and work our way to Budapest. Our final European train would be an express from Venice to London to catch our flight back to the United States. Chris and I planned to go from city to city on trains during the night to save on expenses, and when we spent more than one day in a city, we'd sleep in an inexpensive hostel. We pretty much stuck to this itinerary until we got to Copenhagen, when Chris decided that he wanted to go to northern Germany and Geneva and spend a brief time in Venice, while I wanted to go to Florence and Rome. We decided to split up and go our separate ways before meeting up again in Vienna and from there going on to Budapest.

I completely enjoyed traveling on my own in Europe! Navigating my own travel without an adult's guidance was really liberating. Although most of the people I met in the different cities could speak English, I always tried to learn a phrase or two in each language. I learned to say, "I love you" in the Scandinavian languages and Italian. To be honest, despite my romantic motivation to learn these phrases, I didn't have occasions to use them.

* * *

BIDDING BOXES IN AMSTERDAM

After a quick visit to London, I spent a weekend in Amsterdam, where I played in my first bridge tournament (more on how I relearned to play bridge later). The tournament took place at a youth hostel where I was staying. Since I didn't have a partner to team up with, the administrator of the tournament paired me with Andreas, a man in his late twenties from Germany. We had an hour before play started during which we settled on the conventions and style of card playing we would use. Because we didn't know each other's languages, we relied on hand signals, diagrams, and bridge notations to communicate. While we hashed out our strategy, it dawned on me that bridge was truly another language. Instead of using sentences, we used conventions to get our meanings across. The "language" of bridge, like that of mathematics, is universal, and so simplified the process. Even though we couldn't communicate in our native tongues, this allowed us to develop a common understanding of our bids and card play. However, like different languages, the syntax and convention meanings change depending not only on where you play but also on who your partner is. It was intriguing to learn new, unique conventions and use each at different times. It felt like learning several new languages at once.

When Andreas and I finally agreed on our communication style, we jotted our notes onto a "convention card," required by tournament rules. Our opponents could consult the card when they didn't understand the meaning of our bids. During the bidding process, they were also allowed to ask the bidder's partner for the meaning of a bid. Once play began, only the universal language of bridge reigned. Verbal declarations of a person's bid were not permitted. For questions besides those to clarify a bid, players had to use a "bidding box" to communicate. Bidding boxes are four-sided plastic containers with 35 bidding cards, as well as cards for passes, doubles, and redoubles. They were introduced in Sweden in 1962 to reduce noise in rooms where many bridge games were in session. They also allow for an easy review of the bidding process.

I had never used a bidding box before and, at first, I couldn't get the hang of it. It was frustrating using the box, as the convention was that the box be placed on each person's right side. While I held the playing cards in my left hand, I drew the bidding cards from the box with my weak right hand. Of course, I could have switched hands, but I was stubborn and persisted in doing it normally. The play was conducted in complete silence with the exception of the swish as bidding cards were taken from the bidding box, the occasional inquiry into the meaning of a certain bid, or the stir of a chair when someone went to the restroom. At first, it seemed extremely eerie, and the silence was distracting, but I eventually became accustomed to it and enjoyed how the lack of noise helped me concentrate on the game.

Eight hands before the end of the tournament, my partner and I realized we were so far behind in points that the only possible way we could be sufficiently competitive and finish among the top five partnerships was to play much more daringly. Winning really was only a matter of pride for us since all we could win were master points, which we couldn't use because neither of us were members of a bridge association. We started taking more risks, however remained short on points until the last deal of the tournament. I thought we had sufficient points to reach a very high contract on the last deal. I didn't know how to pull it off, but I really wanted the points. I gulped, and after throwing all bridge rules out of my head, made a weird leap to what I thought the contract should be. With the luck of card location, and, if I might add, skillful play on my end, we succeeded. This was not an altogether kosher way of bidding, yet it happily propelled us to second place in the tournament.

* * *

MORE ADVENTURES IN PARIS

Paris was a pleasure, just as it was the first time I was there. Chris and I stayed with his family in an apartment close to the Luxembourg Gardens. Since we were the only members of the household who knew French, one of our responsibilities was to buy lunch. However, while Chris refused to make the schlep, I was more than happy to go to the butcher shop and bakery alone. This would allow me to practice speaking French.

For three days straight, my task was to buy ham and cheese and baguettes for all of us. I had forgotten how to convert pounds into kilos and tried to remember the formula the first time I was waiting in line at the butcher shop. But I didn't have enough time to figure it out before reaching the front of the line. So, in my semi-perfect French accent, I asked for three kilos of ham, which drew instantaneous bursts of laughter from everyone, those behind the counter as well as those in line. The butcher said that he didn't have that much ham in the store and asked how many slices I wanted. However, when he realized that I didn't understand him, he asked how many people I was buying for. I told him eight and without a word he sliced me sixteen pieces.

On the third morning, when I walked into the shop, the butcher asked me if I was from Spain. When I revealed that I was from the United States, he said, "It's not possible because you don't have an American accent. You must be Spanish!" I told him, "I speak Spanish fluently because I lived in Latin America for many years, but I was born in the United States." As I walked back to the apartment, I was in seventh heaven! He hadn't believed I was an American. What a coup!

A few days later, I bade adieu to Chris, his family, and Paris. My first stop was a return visit to Vichy to deliver the Kennedy half-dollar that I had promised to mail to the maître d'. That night, I went to the disco where I had spent so much time the previous summer. He didn't remember who I was until I handed him the half-dollar he'd requested. I told him, "I didn't mail this to you because I was planning to come back this year to give it to you in person."

His eyes lit up and with a big smile he said, "You remembered. Thank you so much."

We talked for a while about what each of us had done for the last year. He told me that he was taking his exams at the university nearby and then would be looking for a different job. I then strolled around town checking out my old haunts, but one can't return to a city and think that it would remain the same as it was the first time you were there. I had been so looking forward to returning. Dejected, I trudged back to the train station, rode back to Paris, and then boarded the night train to Copenhagen.

＊ ＊ ＊

COPENHAGEN: BEER,
CRACKERS, AND CHALK

When I arrived in Copenhagen, at 11:00 in the morning, Chris was waiting for me on the train platform. We checked in at the hostel before heading to Tivoli Gardens to sip soda and plot our visit. Though both of us were hungry, we were also falling short of our goal of *Europe on $5 a Day*. Our guidebooks gave us a brilliant short-term remedy to save money on lunch: each tour at the Carlsberg Beer factory ended with beer and crackers and cheese! Both of us went to the factory five times, and I continued to go with Oscar, a Swedish friend from the hostel, two additional times after Chris left town.

However, before going to the beer factory and checking into the hostel, Chris and I continued to search our guidebooks to find the hot spots to visit at night. At the top of our list was a five-floor nightclub close to where we sat in Tivoli Gardens. Each floor featured a different type of music. There was slow, waltz-like music on the first floor, 1950s rock and roll on the second, contemporary 1960s sounds on the third, and an all-night hootenanny on the fourth floor. The fifth floor had a dining room. We went on our first night in Copenhagen and, until early the next morning, we moved between the second, third, and fourth floors, dancing with different people and listening to folk music.

I had never been to a hootenanny before and was amazed how people from the audience got up on the stage with their instruments, played and sung their hearts out, and then sat back down to listen to others do the same. That night was the first time I listened to Jesse Fuller's *San Francisco Bay Blues* and, although I was too young to have ever lost a girlfriend when an ocean liner took her away, I immediately connected with the song which might have been a result of my family's move from country to country so many times and leaving so many friends behind when I was younger. Whatever the reason, the combination of the words and mesmerizing cadence drove me out of my mind. When we returned to the hostel, I was happy to find the song on the jukebox along with another song I had never listened to before, Barry McGuire's protest classic *Eve of Destruction* which brought back fond memories of my anti-war and Civil Rights activities back home.

After four days in Copenhagen, Chris was itching to move on to Germany and Switzerland, I, however, was growing tired of constantly going from one place to another. Instead of being on the go nonstop, I wanted to slow down and have a more immersive experience while in Europe. When I had traveled with my family, we always explored a city and its culture over an extended period of time, and while all we had was a month in Europe, I thought that a few more days in Copenhagen wouldn't be a bad idea. And, this might sound corny, but I wanted to stay a little longer in Copenhagen to enjoy its always smiling people and their carefree nature. Chris and I decided to go our separate ways and later to meet at the train station in Vienna to take the train together with his family to Budapest. My plan was to stay in Copenhagen for a few more days and then travel to Florence and Rome before going to Vienna.

The next morning while I was eating breakfast at the hostel, Oscar, who was visiting from Sweden, asked where my friend was. I said, "He went on to see a little of Germany, then he is going to Geneva and Venice. We are going to meet up in Vienna in about a week and a half. How about you? How long will you be staying here?"

Oscar said, "Two or three days, then I'll head up to Oslo before heading home to Stockholm."

Somehow, the conversation turned to money and how both of us were short of it. I asked, "Do you know of anywhere that I can find an easy job?"

He didn't but had a brilliant suggestion, he said, "You and I could buy some chalk and draw pictures on the sidewalk. We'll put a collection box down so people can give us money."

I asked, "Have you ever done that before?"

He said, "No, but some friends of mine have done it. They say that you can get a lot of money in a very short period of time."

"Ok," I said. "let's go buy some chalk!"

He said, "First I have to go up to my room, take off my prosthetic leg, and get my crutches. That way we'll get more money." I was surprised, as I had no idea that he was missing his right leg.

Oscar's prediction about our income intake was correct. By taking off his prosthetic leg, we made the equivalent of $40 a day for three hours of drawing. For two days we drew the same picture with a slightly different theme. We sketched what we called the *Wheel of the World*, including mushroom clouds, farmhouses, airplanes, trains, cars, people with guns, and of course, people with peace signs.

We had fun talking with passersby about the meaning of life depicted in our drawings. To be honest, I don't know whether we made so much money because of my friend's missing a leg or people liked the ideas we were depicting. I tend to think that it was the former, especially the one time we were discussing how to depict our own "eve of destruction" and a priest approached us, patted Oscar on the shoulder, and told him that he should use the money in the box to buy a wheelchair. We felt no shame!

Our routine during the two days that we drew was to draw for three hours in the morning, go back to the hostel so Oscar could put on his prosthetic leg, and take a bus to the Carlsberg brewery at midday for a tour of the Carlsberg factory with beer and cheese, which was our lunch. We'd then return to the hostel so he could take off the prosthetic leg, draw for a few more hours, go back to the hostel for his leg, and spend the evening at a nightclub with our earnings of the day.

* * *

FLORENCE WITH THE PRINCE

When Oscar went off to Oslo, it was time for me to move on to Florence. While I was attracted to the city's architectural and artistic wonders, there was another, more important reason to visit. I wanted to pay homage to the great Renaissance political philosopher Niccolo Machiavelli, who was buried at the Basilica di Santa Croce, and whose short, delicious monograph *The Prince* I had read and discussed with my father the previous summer. Perhaps the first modern political philosopher, and quite controversial for his time, Machiavelli argued that a prince derives power and legitimacy from worldly, secular rather than theological sources. Although the full version of *The Prince* wasn't published until after his death, the sections published during his lifetime were sufficiently provocative and heretical to earn him a reputation for advocating ruthless, corrupt, and tyrannical state leadership. For many philosophers and political scientists, the secular, dispassionate, and factual approach Machiavelli applied to the behaviors of princes was what landed him in jail. For me, Machiavelli's writings marked the beginning of the transition from political thought guided by mysticism and religion to the dominance of rationalism as the basis of political legitimacy. His book also helped me understand Lyndon Johnson's aversion to any dissent against the war in Vietnam, which I saw as a reversion to the mystical.

As I walked across the cobblestoned street toward the church where Machiavelli was buried, I looked up toward the bell tower and was surprised to see a six-pointed Star of David. A tour guide explained that Niccolo Matas, the Jewish architect responsible for the church's facade, had included the star as part of his design. This small fact jarred my preconceptions about Italy as a staunchly conservative Catholic country with very little acceptance of people from other ethnic, religious, or cultural backgrounds. I had mistakenly thought Italy was one big Vatican City. How wrong could I be?

* * *

ROME: CONCERTS
AND THE COLISEUM

As soon as I stepped off the train in Rome, I became aware that my appearance as a Jew, not my physical anomalies, determined how people viewed me. This was shocking since my Jewishness had never crossed my mind until this time in my trip. A porter pushing a cartful of suitcases from the train's baggage car stopped right in front of me as I descended from the train. He asked in Italian, "You're Jewish, aren't you?" My Latin American Spanish helped me understand what he was asking, even though it seemed odd that a stranger would draw this conclusion simply by looking at me. Instinctively, I became defensive, but after a second's thought, I reasoned that different cultures could ascribe different meanings to words and phrases. Maybe, in Italy, this question was not as openly hostile as I assumed, especially since it hadn't been expressed with a sense of malice. Based on this assumption, I responded, in Spanish, "Yes, I am. How did you know?"

He said, "By the shape of your nose."

Interesting, I thought. I had never considered the shape of my nose to be indicative of anything. When he asked, "Can I help you?" I relaxed even more.

"Yes," I said, "could you tell me where the Information Desk is?"

He pointed me in the right direction and off I went. I combed through the Rome section in my guidebook for an activity that would finish close to midnight, after which I planned to sleep on a bench at the train station. When I read about outdoor theaters on the outskirts of town and that the performances finished around 11 p.m., I knew I'd found what I was looking for because it would also take the bus a while to return to the train station. I bought a seat in the last row of one of the large outdoor amphitheaters, where I met a middle-aged couple, Francesca and Marco, who were seated next to me. After they greeted me in Italian, I told them in Spanish that I could not speak Italian. They responded in perfect Spanish, asking where I lived in Spain. They were surprised and interested when I told them that I was from the United States and that I spoke Spanish because I had lived in Latin America for many years.

Switching to English, Francesca asked, "You are Jewish, aren't you?"

This time, I was not disturbed but amused by the question. Why were people so obsessed to find out if I was Jewish?

I quickly responded, "Yes. Is it because of the shape of my nose?"

"No," she said, "it's because of the way you rub your head."

Intrigued, I asked, "And, how does this indicate that I am Jewish?"

Marco answered, "We've seen other Jews rub their temple the same way you do, and we just guessed."

I replied, "Good guess," and I related the similar incident with the porter. They assured me that none of them meant any harm.

They then asked a familiar question, "Why are you in Vietnam?"

"I am not in Vietnam," I replied. "I'm here, and I am against U.S. involvement in Southeast Asia and Vietnam."

Francesca exclaimed, "But you are American! Doesn't everyone in America have to support their government?"

I said, "I do support the government of the United States. I don't support the administration's war in Vietnam."

Francesca continued, "I don't understand how you can make a distinction between your government and the current administration. It's illogical."

It struck me that "government" was the wrong word to use, I said, "There are many people in the United States who love their country but who are working against the injustice perpetuated by the president and his administration," and I recounted the Civil Rights and anti-Vietnam War work I was doing. They said that it would be very dangerous to do the things I was doing in Italy, and continued by telling me stories about Benito Mussolini, the leader of the National Fascist Party during World War II. Before I met them, I was not very aware of Italy's role during the war, even though Mussolini had sent Gino Germani, a good friend of my parents who lived in Buenos Aires, to prison during the war. I made a mental note to start reading about the Italian role in the war. Before the play began, Marco said, "You better watch what you are doing!"

When the play ended, they invited me to a party they were having at their beach house the next weekend, but I had to decline since I'd be in Budapest. I took the bus back to the train station and fell asleep on a bench as planned until early the next morning.

As with my visit to Florence, I had an important personal reason for going to Rome, which had nothing to do with its beauty or its museums. I wanted to see the Roman Forum I'd read about in a biography of Julius Caesar. I decided it would be better to wait until the afternoon to visit the Forum and the Coliseum, so I took a bus tour of Rome in the morning. As soon as I boarded, I realized I was the youngest person and that everyone else was part of a tour group from the United States. Since there wasn't going to be much opportunity for conversation, I sat back and listened to the guide describe Rome's neighborhoods as we traveled through its "seven hills." The few people I did speak with wanted to know if I was touring with a group or traveling solo, where I had been, and where I was going. When I told them that my next destination before heading back to Vermont was Budapest: they warned me not to go or, if I insisted on going, to be extra careful because, after all, it was "an evil country." By this they meant it was a communist country, which was precisely one of the reasons I wanted to go there.

That afternoon, I finally stood in front of the ruins of the old Senate building. I flung my arms out to my side and proclaimed in the words that Julius Caesar used in a letter to the Senate in 47 BC, "Veni, vidi, vici." *I came, I saw, I conquered.* And that, in a nutshell, was exactly what I felt I was doing on my European travels!

∗ ∗ ∗

BUDAPEST:
SURPRISING CONVERSATIONS

I loved Rome and wished I could stay longer, but I had to meet Chris and his family at the Vienna train station for the trip to Budapest. When we finally crossed the Austrian border into Hungary, I was expecting, from what I had been told by other tourists, to smell the stench of oppression, but to my surprise, I didn't sense anything of the kind. Chris and his family were there to visit relatives, so I was left on my own a lot. One morning, as I sat on a bench on Margarita Island in the middle of the Danube between the Buda and the Pest sections of the city reading my guidebook, a middle-aged man sat down beside me. In Hungarian, he said, "Hello."

After saying "Hello" in Hungarian, I said, in English, "I don't know how to speak Hungarian."

He said, in perfect English with a British accent, "Ah, you're British. What city do you come from?"

"No, I'm from the United States."

"We don't get many Americans here! My name is Patrik. Can I ask you a question?"

"Sure, my name is Hank."

"Why are you in Vietnam?"

This initiated a long exchange about differences between the political situations in the United States and Hungary. Contrary to the assumptions of the American tourists I met in Rome, Patrik freely criticized the presence of Russian soldiers in the city. He told me they were confined to their barracks most of the time because many in the country hated their presence. The freeness with which he criticized these political circumstances flew in the face of everything I had learned in my high school class on Marx and Communism. Patrik also said that the country had decided, in the new five-year economic development plan, to renovate much of the public infrastructure that had remained untouched since the 1955 revolution or, in some cases, since the end of World War II.

The crown jewel of the entire European trip was when I met Patrik and some of his co-workers for drinks at a bar later that afternoon. Although their questions were similar to those I was asked in other European countries, the stories they related of their country's travails reinforced a growing belief that I should empathize with another culture and society before forming an opinion, whether positive or negative, about it.

I did not want to return home, but our train passes were almost out of time, money was tight, and the school year was fast approaching.

AN EDUCATION IN AND
OUTSIDE THE MARGINS

Education, both formal and informal, has always played an extremely important role in my life. The reacquisition of the skills I had lost and attaining new knowledge were two constant objectives in my life after the Mexican accident. At seven years of age, after I awoke from my coma, I had no memories of the past and had to rely on others to tell me what I had done and what I knew before the accident. Slowly, over many years, my memory of the past came back. My parents' insistence that I at least attempt to relearn to play the violin and bridge when we returned to New Orleans helped me recover other memories I had lost. In addition to my parents, many of my teachers, whether knowingly or not, were instrumental in helping me regain the knowledge and memories that had faded. My parents insisted that I should be assigned to regular school classrooms instead of special education classes for kids with mental and physical challenges. When a teacher didn't think I was ready to move to the next grade level, my parents would show school administrators the leaps in learning that I had made. Because of their advocacy, I was never held back.

I found certain elements of the learning process difficult, and I still face some of these challenges today. I don't know whether these are the result of the accident or a result of some other factor. For example, I found it difficult to remember the year that the Battle of Waterloo was fought or who was defeated in that battle until I could put it into a social or political context. My recall was near perfect once I pegged it as occurring at the beginning of the Industrial

Revolution, marking the last time or near the last time that opposing armies lined up face to face shooting at each other and the last one standing was declared the winner. It also marked the beginning of guerilla warfare. With that, the summer of 1815, and Napoleon Bonaparte became ingrained in my brain. This process of learning facts was time consuming and I doubt it is the normal way to teach or remember important events and ideas. In my mind, however, eliminating the context of the events would leave out their important contributions to understanding society and becomes an impediment to how we relate to each other.

* * *

NEW ORLEANS: BEGINNING AGAIN

After we returned to New Orleans after the Mexican accident, I started second grade. My school, La Salle Elementary, at the corner of Perrier and Webster Street, was only three blocks from our second-floor apartment in a two-family house at 1324 Webster Street. There was a general sense of community and friendliness among the people in the neighborhood. I often went across the street uninvited to the house under the sprawling oak tree where Martha and Harold, a nice elderly couple who did not have any children, lived for a breakfast of grits, bacon, and eggs with cornbread or a dinner of red beans, pork, and rice. As we settled into our new home, family life, and life in general, started returning to normal.

All the neighborhood elementary-age children, except for the few who went to private schools, attended La Salle, which was located in a three-story brick building with an additional very small fourth floor. The school's lunchroom and indoor play area took up the main floor, while its classrooms were on the second floor, and its administrative offices were on the third floor. Supplies were kept on the fourth floor. A door at the back of the main floor led to an outdoor play area with a jungle gym, a small basketball court and a little grassy area.

On the first day of school, my father and mother assisted me up the stairs to my classroom on the second floor. Walking up the stairs was slow going because of the difficulty I had lifting my right leg, which was not helped by the added weight of the brace. After reaching the classroom door, I waved goodbye to my parents so they wouldn't be there when I entered. The teacher introduced me to the class, which was already seated, and then showed me to my desk. My parents had notified the teacher that I needed to sit close to the blackboard to accommodate my poor eyesight. My parents had also informed both her and the principal that they were planning to help me with my homework because of my poor English.

When it was time for the first recess of the day, I was faced with the daunting task of walking down the stairs I had so arduously climbed earlier. I knew the trip down was going to be much more difficult. We formed two columns on opposite sides of the wide stairway and were told to hold onto the banister while we walked down. I was in the line of kids on the right side. As soon as I got to the top of the stairs, I grabbed onto the right banister with my right hand and slowly stepped down with my right leg. When I lifted my left leg to do the same thing, I lost both my balance and my grip on the railing and immediately fell sideways onto the top step. At that stage of my recovery, taking all my weight on my weak right leg while grasping the railing for balance and stability with my weak right hand wasn't going to cut it.

Birthday party on Webster Street

Almost instantaneously, I figured out how I would have to descend the stairs. The teacher and the entire class watched aghast as I lay down sideways on the stairs and very slowly rolled down. I made sure that I stopped at each stair so that I wouldn't hurt myself. For the next few weeks, until I managed to keep my balance walking downstairs, that was how I always went to recess.

Uncommon behavior like this and my awkward physical appearance made it hard to make friends at school although I eventually made friends. I was often ridiculed, and some students regularly challenged me to fights. Once, some boys from a class above mine started to whip me with their belts during recess. Although they did this with the soft end of the belt, it still hurt. A teacher quickly put an end to this abuse, but not before my harassers had caused welts and bruises on my back. Instead of being punished, the teacher simply told them not to do it again.

I found it frustrating, at first, to keep up with my class work, which went from being a difficult task to seeming almost impossible. As time went by, however, it became much more bearable and easier to do, even though I still struggled to keep up with others in the class. Whatever the task though, I still did the best I could. For example, in the second grade, we had dictation one hour every day. The teacher told us to write using script instead of block letters. I did not yet even know how to write in block letters, much less in script. Not to be outdone by anybody else in class, I opened my notebook to a blank page like everyone else at the beginning of dictation. While all the other students were busily writing down what the teacher was saying, I drew straight lines across the page and started a new page when I saw my classmates do so.

* * *

WHY DO BUTTERFLIES
CHANGE COLORS?

My final report card for second grade year was not the best, which had been expected. My performance was so poor that the teacher recommended I repeat the grade, but my parents convinced the school's administration to let me move on to third grade. Everyone agreed I was advancing rapidly in my cognitive skills, and that it was just a matter of time until I caught up with the rest of my class. My parents continued to work with me at home, which really paid off during third grade, the 1956-57 school year. One day during the first month of that year, our teacher got angry when she realized most of the class hadn't read the science homework for the day. The topic of the unit was how animals adapt to their environment in order to protect themselves from other animals.

She looked at us sternly and exclaimed, "You must all read your assignments on time or else you will not do well in this class. Do you understand?"

There was silence in the classroom, as we all timidly mumbled in unison, "Yes, ma'am."

I was not going to admit to her in front of all my classmates that my mother had read the assignment to me, which would have revealed that I could barely read. I actually was rapidly re-learning to read but was still reading so slowly that by the time I reached the end of a sentence, I had already forgotten the beginning. And, if I'd said that the assignment had been read to me, but I still didn't remember it, I would have been embarrassed that much more. So, I kept my mouth shut.

The teacher quickly regained her composure and challenged us to a contest. "I am going to ask one question and go down each row starting with those whose last names begin with an A and the first person who answers the question correctly without looking in your textbook will receive an "E" for excellence in science on your report card for the entire year. Now, put your books inside your desk. All I want to see on your desks are your hands."

After the class followed her instructions, the teacher began quizzing the students one by one. The science homework question she asked was straightforward: "Why do butterflies change their colors?" Student after student either answered the question incorrectly or simply said that they didn't know the answer. I was seated in the first seat of the second row from the door. I had a crush on Virginia, who was the smartest and prettiest girl in the class and who sat in the very last desk in the row closest to the door. I just knew that she would be able to answer the question.

When the teacher reached me, she asked, "Hankie, do you know the answer to my question?"

I said "No, but Virginia does."

The teacher knew that I was rather intimidated to speak in class, so she added, "C'mon, give it a try."

I remembered my mother reading that part of the book to me and hesitantly started to answer. "So that ... so that they can protect themselves ..."

After the teacher's persistent urging to finish the sentence, I finally said, "Protect themselves from other animals."

To my surprise, that was the correct answer, and I received an "E" for science on my report cards for the entire year! Now that I was guaranteed a good grade, I technically didn't have to do any more science homework for the rest of the year. But that single correct answer was so gratifying, that I was motivated then, and for many years after, to continue to excel in the natural sciences. The moment also meant something else to me. It signified I could do well and didn't have to wait to be told what to do and what not to do. I could do things on my own! What a revelation! Before this win, and since the accident, I wasn't confident about remembering anything when it came to schoolwork. I had just been floating along, doing what people had told me to do, as I had done in the hospital. Because of the teacher's encouragement I realized that I had the ability to answer questions on the spot, and although I could not yet read proficiently, that I was able to understand and recall what was read to me.

On that day I knew I could both dream big and push myself to achieve. I could tame both the mental and physical impairments caused by the accident! My parents were ecstatic when they heard what I'd done in class, and I saw the wheels turning in their minds about how to build on my new-found confidence.

* * *

PICKING UP THE VIOLIN AGAIN

One of my parents' most immediate concerns after my initial recovery was that I relearn to play the violin. Both my father and mother were avid amateur musicians. My father played the violin as part of a string quartet, and my mother had studied piano at the Curtis Institute of Music in Philadelphia. They often played duets together at night before Benjie and I went to bed.

Prior to the accident, my parents had visions of me becoming another young Mozart or Beethoven, and they went to great lengths to fulfill their dreams. When I was only three years old, they asked a violinmaker at the House of Primavera in Philadelphia to make me an eighth-size violin. After many lessons, I could confidently sit behind my father's chair and play along with his string quartet whenever they rehearsed at our house. That dream dissolved after the accident, but my parents now placed another hope in my musical training. They thought that playing the violin would instill a sense of rhythm that would help me sync my body movement so it would be less jerky and more flowing and coordinated. The lessons could also act as a proxy to teach me to read sentences at a more even and rapid pace. Reading music is much like reading a book, and to play in rhythm correctly, you have to be able to read ahead of what you are playing.

Achieving this last goal was difficult because, with my right eyeball locked into the right corner of my eye socket, I had to move my body in order to read ahead. Although I yelled and cursed every time, my parents would say, "You're not reading ahead." I persevered. In what I thought was a crafty solution, I started memorizing the music, thinking I could keep this secret. But when the music teacher stopped me for playing the wrong note and asked what note I was supposed to play, I had no idea where I was on the page! Overall, violin lessons were exhausting and very frustrating. My parents left instructions with the teacher that I should play standing up, which, in my opinion, was the worst! I had to stand for the entire hour with my feet at a 60-degree angle to each other while moving my body back and forth to the rhythm of the music. In addition, the weakness in my right hand and arm made it extremely awkward to hold the violin bow correctly and move it smoothly and forcefully along the strings to avoid making squeaking noises. I continued taking these lessons off-and-on for two-and-a-half years, whenever we were not in Latin America, despite often yelling and refusing to do what either the teacher or my parents told me to do while playing.

BRIDGE

Bridge was a part of my life before the accident, and as mentioned, remained a regular activity into my teenage years and beyond. My first introduction to the game came in New Orleans. My mother and three of her friends, who also had one child each, met one afternoon a week at someone's home for the kids to have a play date. At least, that's what they claimed. More likely, they just wanted to keep us entertained while they played cards and had a few drinks. We would play hide-and-seek or tag outside, but it didn't take long before we grew tired of running around in the stifling New Orleans heat and would start nagging them for something else to do.

Their answer was to set up our own small card table and chairs for bridge next to theirs and a smaller table with Kool-Aid instead of bourbon. They even provided coasters so the condensation from the glasses wouldn't dampen the cards. Every week, little by little, we learned the complicated rules of the game.

Bridge is not, by any stretch of the imagination, an easy card game. It consists of two partnerships challenging each other using a series of card bidding techniques to determine the number of tricks that a partnership thinks it can win. Players sit opposite their partner, and every bid helps a partnership understand the cards that each person has in his or her hand. For example, except in very special circumstances, you can't bid first if you don't have 13 points in your hand. The sequence in which the cards are played can also signal to your partner the number and suit of cards in your hand.

The car accident had completely wiped out all of these lessons from my brain. When my mother and father retaught me the game, they wanted to make sure I could absorb the rules of bidding and playing. The process was therapeutic and a complete success. I loved playing bridge and still do!

After the accident, and once I'd relearned the basics, my mother invited my three friends, along with their mothers, to play cards at our house. Our mothers played in the living room while we played in the guest room.

Bridge was also a source of consolation when I was in high school. I found refuge and acceptance with three other male classmates in a weekly bridge game. This was a new experience because, unlike in Buenos Aires, I was not dependent on my parents for transportation. I could just hop on my bike (the ability to ride being another major accomplishment during my recovery) and ride about 10 to 15 minutes to one of their houses, even if it was on the other side of town. During these games, we spent much of the time arguing about wrong bids or card playing techniques, but also talked about things that happened at school.

* * *

FACING HATE AT HOME

The New Orleans we returned to in the summer of 1958 from Buenos Aires was a changed city because of heated local resistance to the Supreme Court's decisions on *Brown vs. Board of Education I* and *II*. Many residents were angry that the federal courts were monitoring the state's efforts to desegregate public schools and exacting penalties if cities weren't making sufficient strides in these efforts. One of the proposed local solutions was to close all public schools and force families to send their children to private schools, which were not subject to the court's ruling. Obviously, my family was not going to be a party to this effort. While disproportionately aimed at the African American community, the free-floating racial animus focused on any group with characteristics and customs different from the dominant white population. My parents told me the first time they directly encountered the pervasive local racial hatred was in the early 1950s, just after we arrived in New Orleans, when we were the first white family after World War II to have the Ku Klux Klan burn a cross on our front yard. Members of the KKK considered us "white trash" not only because we were Jewish and from the North, but because my father and mother regularly invited African Americans to our house for dinner and other social gatherings.

Discrimination affected me in an even more direct way at times. Cary Rankins, our housekeeper, who was African American and the granddaughter of a slave, was more than a housekeeper to me. Whenever and wherever we were in the United States, whether we were in New Orleans or in Hanover, we would contact her and ask whether she wanted to come live with and work for us. The answer was always, *yes*. She would rent her house in New Orleans and come live with us. Sometimes, when Cary and I returned home from Audubon Park, we sat together in the front of the bus and, because she was not "supposed" to sit in front, people sometimes threw eggs and rocks at us. At the time, it was illegal for African Americans to sit with whites anywhere on public transportation but especially at the front of the bus. Because I did not understand the reason why strangers would throw things at us and especially because my best playmate was Julene, an African American girl, Cary and my parents would often sit in the living room and discuss the meaning and limitations of segregation with me.

Cary and Me

WHITE AS SNOW NEW HAMPSHIRE

Pepina

In February, after we had moved from Buenos Aires to Hanover, New Hampshire, we obtained our next Pepi. The dog belonged to my brother Benjie, who received her as a birthday present when I was in seventh grade. The person my parents bought her from claimed that *she* was male, so we named her Pepi. However, no one could understand why, about three months later, she started rubbing herself against our legs in strange ways. When my parents took her to the vet, we found out she was in heat. So, Pepi became Pepina. Pepina was a Labrador retriever with a slight mix of German shepherd. She had a shiny black coat in the winter that was streaked with brown stripes in the summer. She was very loyal to me.

Once I was riding my bike in the pouring rain to see a movie at Hanover's Nugget Theater. I noticed Pepina running behind my bike. I stopped pedaling and told her to go back home. She turned around with her tail between her legs. I waited until she was out of sight to continue on my way. When I came out of the theater, I was surprised to find her lying, soaking wet, in front of the bikes surrounding mine. She refused to let people get their bikes until I picked up mine. It was a funny scene because everyone knew our dog, and the kids were pleading with her, "Pepina, please let us get our bikes."

We had arrived in Hanover in December 1961 just in time to start the second half of my seventh-grade year in January. The high school included the junior high, grades seven and eight, now often called middle school, and senior high school, grades nine to twelve. It was attached to the elementary school. Promptly at 7:30 on the first day of classes, my mother and I arrived at the student counselor's, Mr. Stimpson's, office. He shook my mother's hand and said, "Please have a seat. Hello, Mrs. Silvert. Hello, Henry."

"Hello, Mr. Stimpson. Call me Hank."

"No, no, no," Mr. Stimpson said, "we can't do that. Hank is too immature a name. From now on, you will be called Henry." He then rubbed his hands together and said, "We must get you into an Ivy League college. What are your plans for college?"

I was still in seventh grade, so I didn't know why he was already talking about college. I didn't even know what an Ivy League college was or that Dartmouth College was one of them.

I told him, "I really don't know if I want to go to an Ivy League College."

He was incredulous and said, "Of course you do, they're the top undergraduate colleges in the United States."

I didn't respond, but it sounded like this was an order because of his uncompromising and aggressive manner. In stubborn silence, I decided I'd never attend an Ivy League college. I did, as mentioned earlier, attend the University of Oxford in England as a graduate student, which has many buildings covered with ivy, but I guess that wasn't his point.

Mr. Stimpson explained that each junior high and high school grade was divided into four tracks, with the first track reserved for Ivy League bound kids. The lower tracks were those deemed suited for lesser-rated colleges. While the subject matter in all tracks was similar for the seventh and eighth grades, the pace of teaching in each track was different. Since none of my assigned classes were for the first track, I didn't think he really thought I was qualified for Ivy League consideration, so I didn't know why he was so adamant that I should attend one. Perhaps he thought that since my father taught at Dartmouth, my parents wanted me to attend an Ivy League college. I don't think they thought this way. They just wanted me to succeed in whatever

I might choose to do. Although all of the other students were in one track throughout junior high and high school, the school made an exception for me because I hadn't received a U.S. education for the previous few years.

The next question Mr. Stimpson asked was, "What foreign language do you want to take when you get to the ninth grade?"

I responded, "Oh, I'd like to take Spanish."

Mr. Stimpson said in rather a condescending voice, "Henry, we don't teach Spanish because anyone who wants to do business with a Latin American can speak in English. They all understand it."

I found it odd and disappointing that they didn't teach the language that I loved, so I asked, "Well, what languages are taught?"

He said, "French and …"

I cut him off, replying, "I'll take that."

* * *

ESTRANGEMENT AND A
SENSE OF ISOLATION

Perhaps because of Hanover's small-town atmosphere, I wasn't immediately welcomed by some of my teachers and classmates. At first, I thought it was primarily due to my limited physical abilities or my difficulty communicating clearly in English. I thought and hoped their reactions would change once they got to know me better. It turned out I was highly mistaken.

While I think these factors certainly affected people's perception of me, I learned shortly after school started there was a much simpler and sinister explanation for my cool reception. People's reactions were based largely on my last name and a stereotypical understanding of my religious background. Not that it should have mattered, but my family was nonobservant except for a few holidays like Chanukah and Passover, and we celebrated these in a nontraditional manner.

The religious hostility fired up the very first week of classes. My chemistry class had an end-of-term test that the teacher urged me to take and do the best I could, even though, she assured me, the grade I received wouldn't count. I was confident that I would do well on the test because chemistry had been one of my favorite subjects at the Argentine International Lincoln School, where I had already completed the year's chemistry class and done very well on the final exam.

When the teacher returned my test the next day, the boy sitting behind me looked over my shoulder and noticed I had received a high score. He tapped me on the shoulder, and, when I turned around, he whispered, "Killer of Christ! Where are your horns? Did you wrap them up under your clothes?" My immediate thought was that he was jealous about my grade. I didn't connect his comments with my parents' explanations of what the Nazi Party stood for when I had walked past its offices in Buenos Aires or the Ku Klux Klan's burning a cross in our front yard in New Orleans. Since I was not raised in a religious environment, it didn't occur to me that he was referring to Judaism in general.

Answering his question, I whispered back in a level voice, "I never met him, so why would I have killed him?" The teacher was, or pretended to be, oblivious to this confrontation. After I recounted this episode to my parents that evening, my mother explained the unfortunate stereotypes of Jews that some people held. She also pointed out that while our family didn't think of Judaism exclusively as a religion, most non-Jews couldn't understand it as anything but a religion. And even then, it should not predispose them to baseless hatred. She suggested I refrain from engaging in conversations about Judaism until I learned more about it. My parents also asked if I wanted them to intervene, but I said, "No, I'll handle it."

The next day, while walking to school along the dirt road, I picked up some small pebbles and stuffed them into my pockets. When I got to chemistry class, I told the boy behind me in a low voice, "If you say anything nasty to me again, I will throw stones at you."

Sure enough, he started haranguing me again about killing Christ and asked me where my horns were hidden. I reached into my pocket for the pebbles and one by one I started throwing them at him. Luckily, the teacher was not in the room to see this, although everyone else did.

He said, "Let's meet at the gasoline station down the block after school and settle this once and for all with our fists."

I said, "Okay," although I had never been in a fistfight before.

When I arrived at the gasoline station, I saw that he had brought his supporters. They formed a circle around us and started cheering him on. Of course, within a few seconds he knocked me down to the ground, sat on top of my stomach, and declared triumphantly, "I won! Give up!"

His supporters started chanting, "Give up! Give up!"

I didn't have any intention of giving up. I said, "No," and started to bite off the buttons of his winter coat. His supporters booed.

He said, "Come on, Henry, you lost."

I said, "No, I didn't," and continued with the buttons.

Eventually, he got off me, and turned and left with his cheering crowd. He also never insulted me again.

During the following months at Hanover High School, I learned that stereotypes such as those held by my classmate and teachers were not always so blatantly stated and were often not directed at me personally. Teachers would often ask questions with hidden meanings instead of saying what they meant. An example of teachers raising important issues but never following through with a full-blown discussion of the topics occurred in my seventh-grade, quarter-long, humanities class. The principal of the high school, Mr. Petrick, taught the class. During a discussion about Rosa Parks and the Civil Rights movement, he asked us to raise our hands if we *wouldn't mind if a Negro family moved onto the block that you lived on*? I doubt most of us had a reference point for this question because there were no African American families living in Hanover at the time. After all, New Hampshire was one of the whitest states in the union. Everyone in the class raised their hand. He continued, "Keep your hand raised if you wouldn't mind if there were two Negro families on your block." A few students lowered their hands. Each time another African American family was added to the block, fewer hands remained raised. Only three of us had our hands up when he asked whether we wouldn't mind being the only white family living on the block. Then, just as the bell rang, Mr. Petrick said, "I just wanted to know."

This stupid statement left me befuddled. Because he persisted, many of the students may have questioned their initial reaction. I didn't know why Mr. Petrick conducted the exercise or what he expected the class to get out of it. His questions did leave me curious about his intentions. I have no recollection of bringing this up with my parents, but to me, it seemed like he wanted to ostracize and shame those whose hands remained raised at the end of the class. At the time, I did not get any notion that this question might also be directed, with a minor change in its wording, to refer to the Jewish community.

It wasn't until eighth grade that I fully understood Mr. Petrick's motive for asking that question. In September 1962, everyone in my eighth-grade earth science class was talking loudly because the teacher, Mr. Garrity, was late for class. When he finally came into the classroom, his face turned a bright red. He stopped dead in his tracks, pointed his index finger straight at me, and yelled, "Henry, shut up!"

I turned toward him incredulously and asked, "No. Why should I be the only one to shut up if everybody else is also talking?"

Mr. Garrity didn't answer. Instead, gritting his teeth, he said, "Get out of here, you dirty Jew bastard."

I didn't think that he meant it and responded "No" again, with a little chuckle.

He then grabbed me by my shirt collar with both hands, which caused me to lose my balance. He dragged me across the floor - with my desk in tow - and out of the room. I didn't understand what had happened and sat furious and crying in the hall for the remainder of the class period. I barely composed myself before I went to my next class, but I did go. I had recovered a little bit more by the time I went home, but all hell broke loose when I told my parents what had occurred. My mother wanted to have the teacher tarred and feathered or, at least, arrested, while my father looked like he was about to burst a blood vessel. They soon cooled down, and my father called Mr. Garrity to get his side of the story.

After the call, my father wrote a long letter to Mr. Petrick, the school's principal and my former humanities teacher, about the incident and telephone conversation with Mr. Garrity that in part read:

Yesterday, September 27th, my son, Henry, was forcefully ejected by Mr. James W. Garrity from his science class, as you know. The nubbin of the matter seems clear enough. Mr. Garrity asked my son to be quiet or leave the class; my son said "no" for whatever may have been his motives at the moment; Mr. Garrity then violently threw him out, grabbing him by the shirt front and tearing his sweater in the process. My son states that he could not keep up with Mr. Garrity and fell before reaching the door, and that Mr. Garrity then dragged him across the threshold; Mr. Garrity made no clear statement to me on the subject. This recitation is for the purpose of showing their areas of agreement; I am making no pseudo-legalistic attempt to get at the "facts" which, as Mr. Garrity said in a telephone conversation, I had with him on the evening of the 27th, must vary with the teacher, the other students, and my son. Nor am I writing this letter to make life difficult for Mr. Garrity or to satisfy the emotions of a stereotypically outraged father. My purpose is somewhat different, and more difficult of expression, for this desire to clarify matters stems directly from my telephone conversation with Mr. Garrity, and not immediately from the incident itself.

My reasons for calling Mr. Garrity were to see how closely to the actual events my son's description of the situation resembled the actual incident so that I could take appropriate home action; to discover Mr. Garrity's reaction so my son could be prepared for a return to his class if that was permissible; and to learn whether it was advisable that I see you or Mr. Stimpson on the matter. When I spoke with him, Mr. Garrity was obviously still upset, and he explained that prior to the incident he was disturbed by the loss of some laboratory equipment and the spilling of acid. I explained to him that Henry had viewed him as his favorite teacher and that a kind of "kidding relationship" had been established between them, at least to the understanding of my son, and that Henry had told me that he thought Mr. Garrity was "kidding" when he asked him to leave the room. For your information, I have never known Henry to defy adult authority outside the home before, and you should know that his own explanation to me of the event included the details about the acid and the missing equipment and his teacher's disturbance. Mr. Garrity told me forcefully on the telephone that my son should have recognized how upset he was. He emphasized that he had told Henry twice to be quiet and was openly defied, and that he—Mr. Garrity—had to maintain discipline in the classroom even if physical violence was called for. (Henry says he was told to leave only once.)

Toward the end of the discussion, I suggested that in a selfish sense the most important thing was for my son to receive a decent education within an environment conducive to his development. Therefore, I asked Mr. Garrity about Henry's reentry to the class and the future relations between the two. Mr. Garrity answered in very gentlemanly fashion that Henry was welcome to return the following day, and that Mr. Garrity had never held any grudges against any student. I have no reason to doubt this statement, and I am confident that it was made in full and generous sincerity. Mr. Garrity also invited me to discuss the matter with you if I so desired. I told him on the telephone that I had no wish to cause undue disturbances if matters could be settled among the three of us. But because in retrospect several aspects of the telephone conversation have left me deeply disturbed, I feel it necessary at least to let my voice be heard in a formal sense.

My primary purpose is to see that some justice be done my son, lest he simply be written off as a nuisance to protect an action which obviously was partially the mistake of the teacher. I think the most pathetic part of it all is that my son gave Mr. Garrity a better shake in telling the story than Mr. Garrity gave him. At least Henry said his teacher was upset, while Mr. Garrity excused himself in part by saying the student should have acted on that knowledge. Why should the teacher expect the student to have the psychological insight, which he himself does not have? Maybe Hankie was upset, too, as Mr. Garrity suggested. If they were both upset, why should the teacher come off the episode excused, my son marked down as at best an impolite boor? Why should Mr. Garrity not have offered me one direct word of apology? Why was I forced to explain some of my son's difficulties, without any reciprocal action from Mr. Garrity in the form of a clear apology for his obvious mistakes? Why should he hesitate to state he dragged Henry on the floor? I was not being punitive or obnoxious on the telephone, and he knew and should know perfectly well I have no intentions of complicating his life. Why should he insult me by sarcastically offering to buy Henry another sweater and have his shirt ironed? I certainly was not insulting him, gushingly excusing my son, or even insisting on my son's version of the story.

The roots of the matter, then, are several. An act of violence was committed by a teacher in a schoolroom; a telephone call by a parent to the teacher contained many elements of genuine goodwill on the part of the teacher, and other of vast defensiveness; the likely outcome if I say nothing is that all will be forgotten except that my son is a juvenile delinquent in the making; a decent human being had been publicly humiliated and his dignity stripped from him before his fellows without a word of contrition from his teacher. Henry has been having his best year in school since the age of six. He was happy, working well, and more alert and brighter than we have seen him in years. To tag him as a behavior problem in a situation, which obviously was not all his fault is to damage the course of his education as well as his recuperation and is to perpetrate an obvious injustice. I have been a teacher myself too long not to know that sometimes students are served up to the Harmon of the system; it happens from kindergarten to the PhD level; in which latter such occurrences are notorious. It is not the first time in your school that Henry has been made to seem a behavior problem because of his reaction to the provocations of others. Last year, after bearing taunts of "fat," "cock-eyed," "stupid" and other such kind remarks from a classmate, he himself reacted noisily and aggressively, and was promptly marked down as a problem child. He is, of course, something of a "problem child," although decreasingly so; but so are those who are the provokers, as well as those adults who lose their self-control, lashing out so at a student with whom there previously had been no difficulties in that class, and who has, to the best of my knowledge so far presented no problems in this still young semester.

As I told you, I am not writing to ask for any hearings, disciplinary action against one or the other or both or even an interview with you. My question is whether, given these circumstances, it is your professional opinion that Henry can well and profitably continue in your school without unjustified stigma. If it is your belief that his dignity cannot be preserved and that a decent and mutually respectful normality cannot be attained, then I should appreciate your utmost of candor in telling me so. The matter is of the greatest importance to me, for involved is clearly the continued growth of my son and the strong possibility that we may be forced to leave the community so that he may start afresh in different and more generous surroundings.

The main reason my father did not mention Mr. Garrity's anti-Semitic remarks was that his concern was to determine whether it was possible for my educational endeavors to flourish at Hanover High School. That he obviously thought this possible in spite of the overt anti-Semitism remains an enigma. However, because of personal experiences with anti-Semitism he tended to be non-confrontational in these types of situations, especially where he had no direct observational knowledge of the event or was uncertain that there were others who would back-up his argument. And, of course, there were only a handful of Jewish families living in town and only one other Jewish student in my grade.

The letter was mailed the following morning. I am not aware of any further contact between my father and the school administration. The afternoon following Mr. Garrity's tirade, the principal's secretary intercepted me and asked me to come to Mr. Petrick's office. Once I was seated opposite him, the principal, the humanities teacher who had so recently asked our thoughts on living next to African Americans, exclaimed, "You know, I would rather live next to a Jew than a Negro." Except, he used a much more objectionable and derogatory word for an African American. There it was racism on a platter.

Mr. Garrity's words the day before and Mr. Petrick's statement were flagrant examples of racism on a platter. Now I understood the purpose of his question in the humanities class. He wanted to give the class a visual image of those who had differing views on this issue in the hope that it would sow division among the students and perhaps influence their thinking. I was amazed, angry, hurt, and astonished by how people could be so cruel. I had never been treated this badly in any school I had ever attended before. Not in New Orleans, not in Chile, and not in Argentina! But here, in Hanover, New Hampshire, where my parents had come to escape the stench of growing racial tension in New Orleans, we had landed in the middle of it. Happily, many of my classmates started to show signs of resistance to these abhorrent statements and overt forms of prejudice.

Another offender though was Mr. Wilson, our eighth-grade geography teacher, who was also one of the town's part-time policemen, and who exhibited a distinct propensity toward racial prejudice and discrimination, although I'm sure he would have vehemently denied this. One day, during our lessons on African geography, Mr. Wilson asked the class, "Where did the Negroid race come from?" There was an audible silence in the classroom.

Nobody said a word, and yet everyone knew that he was about to make an insane remark. "They came from the Niger River," he said; however, he pronounced the name of the river as if it had two g's instead of one. There was absolute silence after he said this, which indicated, to me that my classmates were beginning to understand and reject the implied meanings of what some of the teachers were saying.

* * *

EXPLORING MY JEWISH IDENTITY

After my experience with Mr. Garrity, my parents and I decided I should join a workshop on Jewish history that a Dartmouth student held on Saturday mornings. It examined Judaism from a cultural perspective but also included some references to religion and Jewish philosophy; participants read and discussed parts of the Talmud. There were six people including the instructor in the workshop, but I was the only one who was neither a college student nor an adult. We met on the Dartmouth Green, weather permitting, or at someone's house. I stopped attending these meetings after a few months because there was nobody my age in the group, although I told my parents it was because of the extensive reading required.

While the time I attended the workshop was short, my experience with it proved to be influential in my understanding of history and the emergence of prejudice and discrimination. Until that moment, I thought history was the regurgitation of immutable facts about the past. The readings I did in the workshop suggested that writings of the past were simply, but importantly, different interpretations of social reality. In my mind, understanding historical events from a secular Jewish viewpoint would be different from understanding Jewish history from another point of view, whether that be from a Jewish religious or a non-Jewish perspective. Furthermore, when considering these different perspectives, social facts take on different interpretations and meanings. It dawned on me that the horrific things done to and said about me were expressions of ignorance and fear rooted in different interpretations of history. The question then was how and why did these various interpretations of history emerge? Why didn't I have the same attitudes toward others as they did toward me? Why was the school's principal afraid of living close to an African American while I wasn't? As an eighth grader, I couldn't answer these questions yet.

* * *

A SENSE OF SELF:
MY HIGH SCHOOL YEARS

FORGING AN IDENTITY

Every day during the summer before ninth grade, I dreaded that my experiences in high school wouldn't be any different from those I'd had during the previous two years. Luckily, Mr. Garrity and Mr. Petrick were no longer at the school, thanks to multiple complaints from parents and others about their behavior. And to my delight, once I started high school, my new teachers weren't aggressive toward me. I began to enjoy participating in all my classes.

I had my first exposure to French in the ninth grade. I loved learning to speak French and spent an inordinate amount of time perfecting the correct accent, or at least the teacher's accent. I also liked learning how to use verbs in their proper tense, no doubt inspired by fond and exasperating memories of my mother continually using incorrect tenses in Latin America. I wasn't going to let that happen to me.

Reading and writing French in class was a chore since I could only use my stationary right eye. I also felt intense pressure to read and write faster than I normally would since the other students easily outpaced me. I could read and write easily in the leisure of my own home but the tempo in class was daunting. As with my violin lessons in New Orleans, I tried to memorize what I was going to have to read in class the night before so that it would sound more fluid. Often, however, I didn't know what was going to be read in class, and I'd have to struggle through an unknown passage. When taking an exam, the pressure to speed up was overwhelming. I found it difficult to get the words in my mind onto the paper in front of me as quickly as required and worried that others thought I was stupid. In contrast, I found it difficult to understand how other students were having trouble speaking French.

My troubles with reading and writing weren't limited to French but were prevalent in all my classes. To their credit, some of my teachers understood my difficulties. I don't know whether teachers normally gave people slack on pop quizzes, but one certainly gave me a ton. Mr. Branch, my ninth-grade European history teacher, never scored my quizzes lower or higher than a B+ although I definitively deserved a low grade on most if not all of them.

Despite these pressures, there were spaces where I found a semblance of solace. In ninth grade English, for example, I took inspiration from the famous lines from William Wordsworth's preface to his *Lyrical Ballads*: "Poetry is the spontaneous overflow of powerful feelings: it takes its origin from emotion recollected in tranquility." To me, this quote meant that the creative process wasn't instantaneous nor was it confined to the classroom. It also implied each person's experiences were unique and worthy. I didn't have to constantly compare myself to or seek approval from others for everything I did. My experiences and those of my classmates were equally important to understand, while not necessarily equally valid, and when we shared them with each other, we should always have been open to different interpretations. The notion that creativity emanated from many places and was not limited to schools or other institutions of learning was liberating for me.

"RIGHT-WING, COMMUNIST, FASCIST, PINKO, BASTARD"

Dinner in Norwich, Vermont

During high school, I began to connect the experiences I'd had in the past with current ones. I wondered whether it was possible to move my neighbors to empathize with people they didn't know and who lived in different cultural and political environments. But, on a more personal level, I felt this lack of understanding affected me because I was different from my neighbors in many ways. I had recently moved from the city to the countryside and from Latin America to New England. Moreover, I didn't know the current idioms, lacked close friends, and looked and acted different from everyone else. I started to make a connection between how people treated others in the United States and how they viewed people in other countries, and I began to see how my family and I were often ostracized from community activities because we were seen as not conforming to this country's norms.

To work through this thorny issue, I volunteered in the Civil Rights and anti-Vietnam War efforts that were just starting up in the Hanover/Norwich area. I joined a group that wanted to find out what people in the community really knew about U.S. intervention in the Vietnamese civil war and what they thought about it. I was the only high school student in the group, the others being either college students, faculty, or adult members of the community. After a couple of hours of making random telephone calls, it became clear that very few people knew or cared much about what was happening in Vietnam. We thought that the best way to spark interest in the issue was to have face-to-face conversations with our neighbors and provide them with free literature. I thought that working in groups of two or three would go easily and smoothly, but some of our encounters were extremely testy and dicey. When one man opened the door and saw our peace buttons, he started yelling that we were all a bunch of Russian agitators, called us dirty Communist sons-of-bitches, traitors, and other obscenities before telling us to go back to Russia or Cuba where we belonged. When we began to introduce ourselves, he threatened to call the police unless we immediately left his property. We retreated to the sidewalk, which was not his property, and started relaying our information in a loud voice. He told us that we were still on his property and called the police.

We were in the process of telling him about the tons of napalm that the U.S. Air Force had already dropped on parts of North Vietnam when Mr. Wilson, my racist former geography teacher in his police officer role, pulled up in his police car and told us in a stern, steady, and extremely impolite voice, "Henry, you and your friend must leave these premises, or I will be forced to arrest you." We thanked him for not arresting us on the spot and went to the next house, where we had a fruitful discussion with that neighbor and gave him some informational materials. We continued working like this for three days each week through August, often meeting up with Officer Wilson along the way. I didn't know if we were changing anybody's mind, but the anti-war effort continued to gain steam in our area as it did throughout the rest of the country.

When I began my sophomore year in September, I wanted to continue expanding my knowledge about the war and Civil Rights, but I thought it was odd that none of the teachers, especially the history and social science teachers, brought up issues related to either of these topics. Despite this disconnect, I continued to make connections that linked my schoolwork with the "outside" world.

Many of my classmates didn't agree with my activism for the Civil Rights movement and against the U.S. involvement in the Vietnam civil war. These students awarded me with an honorary title that dogged me until I graduated, "Right-wing, Communist, Fascist, Pinko, Bastard." This phrase confounded me. I had a vague idea of what each of those words meant when used separately, but I couldn't fathom what they were supposed to suggest when connected in this way. Didn't some of them contradict others? I didn't think my accusers got it, other than that they "knew" they should be against people who identified with any of these words. At first, I was very offended when my fellow students muttered the phrase as I walked through the school's hallways. This only confirmed my feeling that people were unwilling to even try to understand the unknown. I eventually decided, "What the hell? I am who I am, and I have just as much right as anybody else to think, say, and work for what I believe." I even began to wear their pejorative phrase as a badge of honor.

* * *

THE BEAUTY AND POWER OF SONG

One morning in the summer of 1963, I went to the Dartmouth bookstore to buy some mysteries, which were my favorite leisure reading because of their scintillating plots and sex scenes. After selecting five books, I wandered to the basement to browse through the music section. I wasn't interested in buying anything. My parents already had quite an extensive collection of classical music LPs. I was just curious to see what was there. In the folk music section, a record caught my eye that transformed my life forever. It was *We Shall Overcome*, a recording of Pete Seeger's June 8, 1963 Carnegie Hall concert. I had never heard of Pete Seeger or listened to folk music. What immediately grabbed my attention, though, was that Seeger, a person from the United States, sang *Guantanamera* in Spanish. Jose Marti, a Cuban poet born in Havana in 1853, wrote the song while living as an exile in New York. I was fascinated that this song was included in an album of U.S. folk songs.

I quickly grabbed the album, paid for it and the mystery stories, and rode home as fast as I could.

Guantanamera was both a protest song about efforts to liberate the island from Spanish rule and a love song evoking the island's beauty. After living for 14 years in exile in New York City, Marti returned to Cuba only to be killed in 1895 while assisting in liberation efforts. I learned that Pete Seeger and other U.S. singers popularized the song in this country as an antidote to anti-Cuban sentiment related to the Cuban revolution. Seeger wanted to use it to create a bond between people in Cuba and people in the United States. I had never heard of a person from the United States who sought to build empathy toward people of another country in this way.

All of the other songs on the album were equally riveting, expressing the hope and determination that we could overcome the xenophobic practices brought on by prejudice and discrimination. The songs brought back memories of injustice in New Orleans, Latin America, and my introduction to life at Hanover High School. The songs gave me hope that I could overcome the limitations forced upon me by heredity and life circumstances.

When Pete sang Neblett's song, *If You Miss Me at the Back of the Bus*, I thought back to when Cary and I had stones thrown at us in New Orleans. His rendition of Tom Paxton's *That's What I Learned in School Today* examined the educational system's tilt toward exalting praise of xenophobia, glorifying the sometimes-violent aspects of U.S. history, while remaining silent on the controversial aspects of its culture. I thought of how the Holocaust and the Argentine Nazi Party were never mentioned in history classes, even at the internationally renowned Lincoln School.

Seeger also sang Malvina Reynold's song *Little Boxes* about the increasing pace of suburbanization and homogenization of U.S. culture, which reminded me of the exclusive expatriate enclaves in Buenos Aires. Even his inclusion of Woody Guthrie's song, *Mail Myself to You*, about a young person who puts a stamp on his or her forehead to be mailed to a loved one, made me think of when my parents had sent me to visit Manuel and Beulah for a month during the summer of my rough time at junior high school.

All of the songs on the album gave me a feeling of hope and a sense of belonging to a broader community that I had never experienced. I felt close not only to those living near me but to those in distant places who shared my desire to live in a world free of prejudice and discrimination. I was so enamored with the album that I listened to it almost every day, which drove the rest of my family crazy.

* * *

SOPHOMORE YEAR
AND PEANUT BUTTER

If I wasn't making friends with my classmates, at least I still thought many of the things we were doing in my classes exciting. Since the accident, I had been hard-pressed to be able to provide detailed, well-structured, and chronological descriptions of the sequence of steps needed in order to accomplish a task. One assignment in English, helped me overcome this shortcoming. Our teacher, Mr. Orenstein, gave us the following assignment: *Write a detailed recipe for a peanut butter and jelly sandwich for a person who has never made a sandwich before.* Everybody laughed at what we thought was such an easy assignment. The day after we handed in our recipes, Mr. Orenstein started class by placing three jars of peanut butter, three jars of jelly, two small plastic bags, three loaves of white bread, a roll of paper towels, utensils, and a bottle of water on his desk. After he arranged everything, he proceeded to make sandwiches using our recipes. One recipe was very simple; "Take a piece of bread, put the peanut butter on it, take the jelly and put it on the peanut butter, and put another slice of bread on top." So, Mr. Orenstein took a slice of bread and put it on top of the paper towel in the center of his desk. Next, he took a jar of peanut butter and put it on top of the slice of bread. Then he took a jar of jelly, put it on top of the jar of peanut butter, and then put a slice of bread on top of the jar of jelly. The entire class was in stitches. Another recipe called for peanut butter to be spread on a piece of bread, jelly to be spread over it, and then covered with another piece of bread. Mr. Orenstein dutifully took a piece of bread, dipped two fingers into a jar of peanut butter, spread the peanut butter on the *six sides* of the bread, spread the jelly on top of the peanut butter, again on all six sides, and balanced another piece of bread on one of the sides of the first piece of bread. After cleaning his hands with the bottled water, Mr. Orenstein moved onto the next recipe. This went on until he had made sandwiches using all the recipes. Everyone in class was stunned, but we also had a better understanding of the importance of being detail oriented and focusing our attention on the instructions for an assignment. Our next homework assignment was to revise our recipes.

Mr. Orenstein's example made a big impression on me. Of course, it was very important for recipes to be concise. In the broader context, a focus on written details was also needed to minimize the reader's misinterpretations. It dawned on me that I was already doing this in my Civil Rights and anti-war activities when it was necessary to follow instructions on how to conduct a telephone interview, ask for volunteers, or call to ask for contributions. Our group didn't have a guide for door-to-door canvassing or the steps we should take if we were arrested. I brought this issue up at one of our meetings and we set about writing out the steps to follow in various situations. This collaborative effort proved to be both beneficial and informative. For example, I had no idea that we had legal counsel and a phone number to call other than that of our headquarters if we encountered any legal trouble.

* * *

CATCH-22

I was drawn to books that questioned authority or viewed reality from a wildly different viewpoint. I also enjoyed humorous interpretations of dire situations that gave a sense of life's endless possibilities. Of all the books I read during this time, only one had all of these elements. When Mr. Orenstein gave us a list of novels to choose from for an oral book report, I selected *Catch-22* without really knowing much about it. Joseph Heller's novel chronicles the fortunes and misfortunes of Yossarian, a bombardier in the U.S. Air Force stationed off the coast of Italy during World War II. Once I started the book, it was impossible to stop reading because I found it so engrossing. It was the first contemporary anti-war novel I'd read. In an especially comedic manner, *Catch-22* depicted the lunacies of war and the bureaucracy that supported it. As I continued to read into the wee hours of the morning, I kept laughing out loud. Fortunately, my mother and father were usually up late, and my brothers slept with their doors closed.

One of the many "catches" of the novel is that a person who was crazy couldn't go on bombing missions, but if you told your commanding officer you were insane, you were obviously not crazy because only crazy people willingly went on these missions. What was Yossarian to do? He decided to feign a liver illness that couldn't be diagnosed properly. Whenever he told his commanders it flared up, they sent him to the infirmary until the "symptoms" resolved. I started to laugh during my oral presentation as I described how Yossarian passed time in the infirmary censoring letters of other airmen to their families and loved ones back home. Nor could I stop giggling when I described how he would, on different days, declare war on different parts of grammar in these letters. On some days, he would black out all adjectives, while on others it would be all pronouns. But the novel also had a more somber message. The catch of all the catches was that every time an airman reached the maximum bombing missions needed to go home, the Air Force would increase the quota. In the end, Yossarian decides to desert the military by following his friend Orr who, after crash landing in the Mediterranean, rowed himself to Sweden in the plane's inflatable lifeboat. Yossarian ends up going to Sweden by land instead of by sea.

For me, one of the most haunting aspects of the novel was the juxtaposition of the individual against a crazy collective. Yossarian says throughout the novel "They're trying to kill me," which, in a certain way, was accurate. In the context of the novel, this was extremely powerful, as dying in war is applicable to all and is indiscriminate. For the general population, people become commodities and the dead cease to have any real meaning to anyone except to relatives or friends. For Yossarian, the "they" he refers to are more concerned with winning a war than they are with who was killed in it. After all, Yossarian was only a pawn on a chessboard. Because of my stellar reputation as a troublemaker, I was pleasantly surprised that my book review was so well received!

INTRO TO EXISTENTIALISM

Some of my other classes also made an impression. In French class, we read Albert Camus's *The Stranger*, whose main character, Meursault, is in a perpetual state of denial because of his rejection of society's norms. I sympathized with his alienation since I felt the values of those around me were inconsistent with mine. I personalized Meursault's views—I was interested in combating fruitless foreign wars and unjust policies in the United States while others focused only on local and church-related issues. However, I never felt, as I thought Camus might have, that we should just accept these differences and not work to change them. While Meursault never commits suicide, he definitely accepts it as one predetermined outcome of his life experiences. I thought that Meursault's state of mind resembled Emile Durkheim's concept of anomie, a feeling of isolation caused by the rapid speed of change in modern society. I believed that in a modern society, human beings are the designers of their own destiny, so the novel's concept of predestination seemed absurd. But, of course, that was Camus's philosophy.

CASSIRER

Kitchen Debate

As my junior year of high school rapidly approached, my father devised a scheme to get me into the "studying" mood. He suggested I read and discuss some of his favorite books with him, beginning with Ernst Cassirer's *Myth of the State*. He thought the book would help me see the different ways people understand the "value of people" and political processes. The book was Cassirer's attempt to comprehend the transformation of the state that Adolph Hitler envisioned, which supplanted rational argumentation, skeptical and critical objections, and discussion of polities and political practices with an emotional belief in divine political intervention that could only be achieved by stifling all political inquiry and dissent.

I was struck by how he presented the historical ebb and flow of these concepts, starting with the political philosophy of the ancient Greeks. Cassirer revealed the long-standing tension between the understanding of human activity using irrational, mythical, and otherworldly beliefs, and a conception of rationalism and scientific understandings as the driving force of development. For him, Germany's Nazism and Italy's Fascism represented a return to mythical beliefs about a people and a country's destiny.

Once I finished the book, my father and I considered how this interpretation of political history applied to the current situation in the United States. Could the tension between rationalism and emotionalism assist in understanding the increasing polarization of views in the United States between those who wanted to expand political and economic participation to a continually larger portion of the population and those who didn't want this to occur? While our discussions were mostly intellectual and based largely on the readings my father provided, I lacked the concrete historical knowledge my father possessed to back up my arguments. Instead, my findings were based on my father's arguments, rather than my own interpretation of the past. At that point in time, I wasn't prepared to make a final argument about whether the United States was headed toward totalitarianism.

* * *

JUNIOR YEAR

I was looking forward to starting eleventh grade after the intellectual discussions I'd had with my father about the books I read, but my classes seemed rather mundane and didn't relate at all to my anti-war and Civil Rights work and other issues I thought important. This was particularly true of a section of my English class where we read the Bible, including both the Old and the New Testaments. I raised my hand when I understood this to be the intended course of study and asked, "Isn't there a separation between church and state in the United States? The Bible is a religious text."

The teacher, Mr. Larry replied, "Yes Henry, you're right but we are reading the Bible as a piece of great literature, not in a religious sense."

I was unconvinced, but what could I do? The voice of authority had spoken. Since I thought the unit was an excuse to bring religion into a public-school classroom, I simply refused to read the text. Instead, I surreptitiously read Mary McCarthy's *The Group*. I kept the Bible on top of my desk open to the page we were discussing and McCarthy's book on my lap. I wasn't sure this fooled Mr. Larry because he would occasionally ask me, especially during the reading of the Old Testament, "Henry, isn't that right?"

I always answered, "Yes, sir," and went back to reading my novel. I had no idea whether my answer was right or wrong because he would simply go back to his Bible discussion. Every day we had a short pop quiz on the material we were supposed to have read the previous night. Betty, the girl who sat next to me in class, and I were supposed to exchange test papers and grade each other's quizzes as Mr. Larry read the answers. We never exchanged them and just wrote in the correct answer as the teacher provided them. Sometimes we left the answers blank just to show that we didn't know everything about the Bible, which, of course, was more than accurate. This was not the quality of teaching I expected in English class after the hilarious episode with Orenstein's peanut butter sandwiches and the liberation I felt when I read Wordsworth's simple definition of poetry. But I did find *The Group* quite exhilarating and a tad raunchy!

* * *

OPENING HORIZONS

The United States (or American) history class was a watershed for me. Our teacher, Mr. Murphy, encouraged the class to connect current events with the past. One of the class requirements was a daily subscription to the *New York Times*, and we had to read the first page every morning. He also assigned articles that examined the same events in U.S. history from different points of view.

I was already a regular newspaper reader, as perusing the paper at the breakfast table was a long-standing tradition in our family. In Buenos Aires or Santiago, the national paper was delivered to our door, but whether we were in New Orleans or Hanover, we always subscribed to the *Times*, and I read it while eating breakfast with my parents. Now that I had my own subscription, I didn't have to fight to get the sections I wanted to read. Reading only the first page was a breeze but it wasn't really satisfying since the meat of the articles was usually found in the back pages. Journalists couldn't possibly squeeze everything onto the first page. And what about the stories that never made the front page and were sometimes much more interesting? The editorial and op-ed pages usually provided great interpretations of news articles on the first page. Weren't they also valuable? And what about my favorites, the daily articles about bridge and sports, especially those about my favorite teams, the New York Yankees and the Green Bay Packers? I would devour the entire first section of the newspaper in the morning and the rest during study hall at school if I wasn't quietly arguing politics with Sally, the girl who sat next to me.

Mr. Murphy gave us a pop quiz on the contents of the first page every morning. After taking several of these quizzes, it dawned on everyone that he had tricked us. To get a perfect score, we had to have read the continuation of the articles inside the first section of the paper. Since I already did this, it was a win-win for me.

The two most prominent topics on the front page were U.S. foreign policy, especially in Vietnam, and race relations inside the United States. Mr. Murphy avoided issues concerning the conflict in Southeast Asia and the current Civil Rights movement as he considered them too current to be viewed as history. He did spend a lot of time on the U.S. Civil War, assigning many articles analyzing it from different perspectives, many of which challenged our understanding that its sole purpose was a humanitarian desire to end slavery in the Confederate states.

In addition to learning about the fervent abolitionist sentiment among some segments of the population, we discovered the economic argument that the war was primarily a result of the unequal cost of goods and services between the Confederacy and the Union. While the immediate effect of the Civil War was to abolish slavery, its long-term impact was to create a united and free labor force that could compete for fair wages throughout the country. For example, the advantage that Southern states had before the war in ship-building disappeared once they could no longer use slave labor.

Although it fascinated me that pressing economic issues rather than simply an opposition to slavery resulted in the Civil War, these articles presented the supremacy of economic issues as a fact or a foregone conclusion, not as a hypothesis to be worked out, and I just didn't get it at the time. I thought, however, the answer might be found in a new course that the high school was offering entitled Marx and Communism. The class was only offered to tenth graders but the teacher, Mr. Thoms, knew my reputation as a rabble-rouser and, with the school and my parent's permission, allowed me to audit the class. It was the first time that I'd ever read anything directly related to communism, including Karl Marx's, *Communist Manifesto*, and excerpts from his and Frederick Engel's, *The German Ideology*. The class provided little background information about where Marx got his ideas. It was mainly a history class that explored some of Marx's writings and the effects they had on the world. While the class allowed us to look at the world through another person's conceptual framework, it was neutral on the frameworks behind the communist experiments around the globe.

MY FATHER'S PROTÉGÉ

My father and mother had thousands of books, in both English and Spanish. While most were academic, there was also a sizeable amount of fiction and poetry scattered among bookshelves throughout the house, including one room in our barn. It was while rummaging through some bookcases in the living room that I stumbled on a book of poetry by Dorothy Parker. As I started to read, I found the book difficult to put down, and I continued reading until I finished the last poem. One poem in particular caught my attention because it mirrored my feelings at the time:

> *If I had a shiny gun*
> *I could have a world of fun*
> *Speeding bullets through the brains*
> *Of the folk who give me pains*

Although I abhorred guns, these were, in principle, my sentiments exactly!

Another of Parker's poems that caught my fancy, probably because I was in my teens, was *Men Seldom Make Passes at Girls Who Wear Glasses*. In a signed comment underneath the poem, my mother answered, "But girls seldom wear glasses in bed." Another living room find was Howard Fast's 1944 novel *Freedom Road*. I consumed the book in one day, and eventually used it as the source for a book report for English class. Fast's novel was a riveting recount of the prejudice and discrimination that built up during Reconstruction and led to the formation of the Charleston, South Carolina branch of the Ku Klux Klan. His depiction of Southern life brought back memories of my experiences in New Orleans, as well as how different it was living in Latin American countries where, it appeared to me, there was more integration of people from different racial backgrounds.

* * *

GETTING SERIOUS

When I returned from my month traveling around Europe with Chris, my father, sensing my boredom, suggested that I read some books written by European philosophers that might help me better appreciate the excitement I'd felt during my travels. He also suggested that some of these books might help me understand current events. The reading list included some of the European philosophers of the Enlightenment, including Thomas Hobbes's *Leviathan*, John Locke's *Second Treatise*, and Jean-Jacques Rousseau's *Social Contract*. Since I had been so infatuated with my journey to Hungary, he also included Karl Marx's *The German Ideology* in its entirety, not simply the excerpts assigned in class. Although my father was always available to discuss the books, he encouraged me to read the interpretations of those works in George Holland Sabine's anthology, *A History of Political Theory*, whenever I thought the reading was getting too "over my head" or confusing. Sabine's book, much like Cassirer's, covered the period from the Greek philosophers until Fascism and Nazism in the 1930s. Unlike Cassirer, it didn't weave a story about the flow of philosophic views but analyzed each person's ideas solely from his own perspective. Summer vacation was nearly over, so we decided to prolong reading the list for my entire senior year.

Each of these thinkers presented a different conception of how human beings relate to each other, which only led to more questions:

Was it necessary, as Hobbes proposed, for human beings to surrender their freedoms to an absolute monarch to protect themselves from their violent, natural tendency to be in a brutal struggle of a war of all against all?

Were people peaceful and trustworthy enough, as Locke wrote, to empower a monarch to arbitrate when disagreements arose concerning their natural right to life, liberty, and property?

Were people, according to Rousseau, compassionate and honorable yet fearful of others and obsessed with self-preservation? Did laws and regulations only become necessary when people became dependent on one another?

Did human beings only form groups, as Marx wrote, because of their need to produce their food and shelter as well as to reproduce?

Besides the overwhelming complexity of the issues that each of these thinkers wrote about, I felt that their positions must have something to do with the social, economic, and political transformations that were occurring when they were alive. The move from rural to urban living, the increased commerce between different regions of the world, and the shift from the dominance of a religious outlook to a secular one all played a role in their thinking.

I could understand why Hobbes, an Englishman born in 1588, during the heyday of the Protestant Reformation, was consumed with ways to clamp down on unrest and thought that anarchy could only be avoided with people's allegiance to a strong monarch. On the other hand, Locke, also an Englishman, born half a century after Hobbes in 1632, was more focused on the aftermath of this Reformation and how a monarch could preserve people's life, liberty, and property. Certainly, he, more vividly than Hobbes, saw the effects of this transformation on the erosion of the importance of feudal estates and the growth of cities and commerce. Rousseau, born in Switzerland in 1712, eight years after Locke died, argued that a monarch was only necessary to help develop laws and regulations to help ferret out the differences between people who otherwise had good intentions. These three political philosophers were grappling with the problems related to human beings moving from a state of isolation to the development of a political structure or, in their terms, a social contract. Marx, born in 1818 at the beginning of the Industrial Revolution in Europe, questioned whether it was possible that human beings had ever lived in a state of nature. He wondered how human beings could develop the sustenance of life in isolation, without living, from the very beginning, in groups? Yes, people could find food alone and develop a form of shelter alone, but how could they reproduce alone? The key to his thinking was the third ingredient, the need to reproduce, was necessary for human beings to survive. People always had to live in groups to survive. Therefore, to argue that human beings needed a monarch because at one time they lived in a state of nature and needed protection from one another was, for Marx, preposterous. There must be some other reason for having a government. While Marx's interpretation of human history piqued my imagination in a way the others did not, I wasn't yet in command of the information I needed to fully support his position.

* * *

A SERIES OF FIRSTS

Senior year was my best, socially and academically.

TWIST FOR TWO

Every Friday night, the high school sponsored a student dance in the school's cafeteria. It always featured a live band, usually composed of students from our school, but sometimes from a nearby high school. Seventh and eighth graders were not allowed to attend because they had dance classes on Thursdays after school, which were also conducted in the school cafeteria. And, yes, I'd gone to those classes, too. The girls would sit against one of the walls and the boys would sit against the opposite one. Boys and girls rotated in choosing their partners for each dance. This worked well for everyone except me because nobody wanted to dance with someone who limped and had a right eye that couldn't move. Lucky for me, there were an equal number of boys and girls in the class so that someone got "stuck" with me unless, which sometimes happened, they chose to sit out that dance.

I regularly attended the Friday night high school dances until I graduated. While there were many ninth to eleventh grade girls who didn't have dates and whom I could dance with while I was an underclassman, twelfth grade was different. Dating was now the name of the game and, while I had never been on a date before, I was eager to participate. My basic problem was that I was really shy and felt awkward about asking a girl on a date. I couldn't understand how other guys could just walk up to girls and be so cool and debonair. I had to overcome my fears. So, on a Monday morning in January, I asked Amy, an eleventh grader from my carpool, "Would you like to come with me to the Friday night dance?"

She said, "I don't go on dates."

"Ah, come on, it will be fun."

"Well, maybe but, I'll have to ask my parents for permission."

"Oh ..."

"Can I let you know tomorrow morning? If I can go, how will we get there and back?" That was a good question because my parents wouldn't let me take the tenth-grade driving class due to the accident in Mexico. Thinking quickly, I replied, "Oh, my mother will drive us there and back."

The next day in the carpool, Amy said, "I can go to the dance with you, but my mother said that I have to be home by 9:30 sharp."

"Great, I'll pick you up at 6:30."

When I went to pick up Amy on Friday night, her mother opened the door and said, "Hi, Henry, come in out of the cold." She turned and shouted up the stairs, "Amy, Henry is here."

Then sternly looking at me, she said, "Amy must be back by 9:30! Don't be late!"

I sheepishly replied, "Alright," but her words filled me with fear. My mother never arrived anywhere on time. How was I going to get her to pick us up at the dance with enough time to get Amy home by 9:30? I remembered the many times she'd double park on the crowded streets in Buenos Aires and say, "Wait here, I'll be back in just a minute." This often meant, "Wait here. I'll be back in anywhere between five minutes and two hours."

During the short drive to the school, my mother, realizing that I was tongue-tied, chatted with Amy asking about how long she had lived in Norwich, how she liked her classes, and what she liked to do in her spare time.

As we approached the school, I interrupted and said, "Mommy, could you pick us up at 9:15? Amy's mother says that she must be home by 9:30."

"Sure, Hankie!" Nobody at school knew that my nickname was Hank or its diminutive form. Amy looked at me quizzically, but I was more concerned that my mother wouldn't be back by 9:15. There was nothing more I could do.

When we entered the cafeteria, the band was playing a slow tune. I asked, "Amy, shall we dance?"

Amy said, "Oh, no, I don't slow dance. I'll be right back." Off she went to speak with some of her friends. I was left watching others dance.

Fifteen minutes later, when the band was playing a twist, she came back and said, "Let's dance." We twisted for a while. During a break, I asked, "Do you ski much during the winter?"

Amy said, "Oh, yes. I ski on Mondays and Wednesdays and both days on the weekends. You know, I'm on the Hanover High ski team." I hadn't known any of this. She continued, "Do you ski?"

"No, I don't."

"You should learn. It's really fun!"

I was too embarrassed to tell her about the time I'd fallen and couldn't get up when I tried to learn to ski at the Dartmouth ski slope in Lyme, New Hampshire. After a long and tortuous effort to get both skis on my feet, I fell sideways on a small incline in the snow and didn't have the strength in my arms or my legs to hoist myself up again. That quickly put an end to my skiing career. As we talked, I began to realize that it wasn't enough to ask just anyone out on a date. There had to be at least a smidgeon of chemistry and shared interests as well. The clock was ticking, and it was getting close to time for us to leave. Surprise! My mother did show up at 9:15. On our way back, I sat next to my mother and Amy sat in the window seat. As soon as we stopped at Amy's door, she said goodbye, and ran into her house. I didn't even get a chance to give her a kiss on her cheek. The date was a disaster, but at least I had finally asked someone out.

FINALLY

My first kiss came toward the end of the school year at the Senior Prom. Somewhat bummed out about my first date, I didn't ask anyone to the prom. I walked into the auditorium and saw that many people had dates, but, like myself, there were some who didn't. I went across the dance floor to a friend of mine from English class who was standing alone.

"Hi, Ruth. How are you?"

"I'm fine."

"Did you come with anyone?"

"No, I came alone."

"I didn't come with anyone either." After a few seconds of uneasy silence that seemed to last an eternity, I added, "Would you like some punch?"

"No, thank you. I'm alright."

"The place is decorated nicely, isn't it?"

"Yes."

"And the band is playing great music. Would you like to dance?"

Ruth just nodded and we walked onto the dance floor and started twisting to *Twist and Shout*. We then started dancing to rock and roll songs like *Johnny B. Goode* and *Louie Louie*. Our eyes never lost contact, and there was no need to talk while dancing. I loved dancing to rock and roll as it allowed for all sorts of fancy movements and I could still hold hands with my partner.

We danced nonstop for 45 minutes and then went outside for some fresh air to cool down.

I said, "I like dancing with you."

"Same here. It gets very hot in there with all those people."

"Yes, but we were dancing a lot! I hope I didn't hurt you when I stepped on your foot."

"Oh, no. You hardly hit it."

"This was the first time that I danced to rock and roll music holding someone's hand and my feet got all tangled up."

After dancing some more, we sat down in a stairwell close to the auditorium and talked. She took my hand and I leaned over and kissed her on the lips, and then a second one, and a third one. Shortly after that, we wrapped our arms around each other and were in a long, deep, and lovely French kiss. It was bliss! At the same time, I was disappointed; I had just met someone I wanted to get to know better yet would be leaving in September to attend New York University.

* * *

STONED

Senior year was also the first time that I smoked marijuana. Some of us occasionally crashed Dartmouth College dances on Saturday nights. Most of the Dartmouth College students at these dances brought dates from other colleges (the college wasn't coed yet), but some dated high school girls. One Saturday night, my friend Jeff and I bought some marijuana from a Dartmouth student and then went down to the pier on the Connecticut River to smoke. We sat on the dock, with our feet dangling over the water. After Jeff rolled the joint, he lit it and took a puff.

"Here," he said, holding his breath as he handed it to me.

I took a hit before handing it back to him and said, "I don't get what the rage is all about. I don't feel anything!"

"You've got to inhale and hold your breath for a few seconds for it to work. It's like a cigarette. Here, let me show you."

I'd never smoked cigarettes so, after inhaling, I went into a coughing fit. Before we headed back to the dance, I did get a buzz. We had some difficulty keeping our balance walking back up the hill, but we finally made it. When I finally felt like I could maintain my balance, I rode my bike home. That was the only time in high school that I smoked anything.

STATISTICALLY SPEAKING

In my senior year, Ford Daley, the teacher of the Science Issues and Research class, asked me if I'd like to take an advanced science class the school was offering. All ten students in the class would be responsible for completing a scientific project of their own choosing during the year. Classroom assignments were readings and experiments about the history of science. At the very least, I would be able to get a whiff of what my parents had been doing all those years. Even more enticing, everyone who completed the project and classwork would be guaranteed an A for the course no matter how their project turned out.

On the first day of class, Mr. Daley pointed out that the term *science* didn't refer only to the natural sciences, such as biology, chemistry, and physics, but also included the social sciences, such as sociology, political science, economics, and psychology, which studied individuals, groups, societies, and nations. Through our reading of the historical development of scientific knowledge, we learned that both the natural and social sciences use a singular, systematic, approach to their subject matter called the *scientific method*. Researchers' use of the scientific method allows others to replicate their studies, which creates a sense of constancy and allows for generalization. A one-time discovery could either mean that the study's finding occurred by accident or the researcher's hypotheses had been interpreted inaccurately.

To drive this idea home, Mr. Daley challenged us to replicate a finding—the time it takes for an air bubble to rise to the surface of liquids depends on the density of those liquids. Our task was to reconstruct the experiment and either verify or falsify the finding. Mr. Daley had beakers, containers of molasses, air hoses, a pump, and stopwatches available in the science lab and asked us to develop a way to test this finding. After discussing in pairs how we would go about doing this, the class came together and decided on a common strategy. We would divide into five pairs, and each pair would set up six different sized beakers so that they wouldn't fall to the side. Each group would then attach the same sized air hoses to the bottom of each beaker and fill the beakers with molasses. Next, we'd use the pump to blow air into the hoses and record the time it took for the air to reach the top of the molasses. In the final step, each pair would separately write its findings and we would then combine them into one report.

The experiment was fun and a great hands-on learning experience. But what were we to do with all that tasty molasses once the experiment was over? Without informing Mr. Daley, we decided to make rum with it. We emptied all our small beakers into the biggest beaker in the laboratory, put it into an incubator, and set the timer for two weeks. Although nobody thought we could keep this hidden from Mr. Daley, he never showed any signs that he knew what we had done. Two weeks later, we stayed after school to distill the molasses. After making sure that the result did not contain wood alcohol, which we'd read was deadly and could blind us, we divided the rum among ourselves and drank it. There wasn't enough rum for any of us to get drunk after we'd split it between the 10 of us, but it was better than you'd expect!

* * *

GETTING STARTED

The time had come for us to choose our research question. Most of the students in the class were interested in natural science projects, like extracting the DNA molecule from a spinach leaf or the impact on men of a spouse's menopause. I was at a loss for a viable topic and research question. Then I remembered Tom Lehrer's song *Pollution* from his 1965 album "That Was the Year That Was."

I was sure that the American cities Tom Lehrer referred to were big cities like New York, Chicago, and Los Angeles, but I wondered whether pollution also affected people in smaller towns, like Hanover. I didn't think that there was air pollution in Hanover, so I felt that wouldn't be a fruitful question to research. I had heard rumors that swimming and fishing were prohibited in the Connecticut River, so maybe I could focus on water pollution. Memories from my anti-war activity suggested that proximity to an issue meant more people were aware there was a problem and, those that were, exhibited a greater willingness to talk about it.

My central questions, then, were to determine whether people living in Hanover perceived a water pollution problem, and, if so, what were they willing to do about it. At Mr. Daley's suggestion, I combed through the school's small library searching for articles on water pollution either in Hanover or in the United States. To my chagrin, there were very few articles addressing the issue in the United States, and none that used survey data. There were no articles addressing water pollution in the Hanover area. I was somewhat deflated about these findings, however, the next day in class, Mr. Daley excitedly said, "That's great, Henry! Don't give up. That means that you are doing original research. Tomorrow, why don't you go back to the library and see whether there is anything written on what influences people's perceptions?" This cheered me up a little, but I couldn't understand how I was supposed to develop my hypothesis if there was no prior literature.

My parents came to my aid and asked me what I thought were the major differences between cities and towns. Annoyed, I yelled, "I don't know!"

My mother said, "Hankie, calm down."

"Okay."

"Do you recall the first thing that you thought when we first got here?"

"Yes."

"And what was that?"

"That there were no people."

"You mean that there were fewer people than in other places that we lived. Do you think that there is air and water pollution in cities with more people than in Hanover?"

"Ok, mommy, I don't know!"

"C'mon, Hankie. Think hard."

"Yes, there is."

"What newspaper did Mr. Murphy make you read?"

"The *New York Times*."

"And what newspaper do most people read in Hanover?"

"*The Valley News.*"

"Why do you think that Mr. Murphy didn't have you read the local paper?"

"Well, I guess he wanted us to learn something about things that occur outside of this area."

"Right! So, would you say that people in small towns might not be as informed or concerned about national issues than those who have better and easier access to newspapers that report on national issues?"

"So, you're saying that people in small towns are less informed than those in cities."

"No, I'm not saying that at all. But you might make a guess that people in Hanover would not perceive water pollution to be an important issue to address because it is a small, insulated area."

"But you just said that this was not what you said."

Calmly, my mother continued, "Remember, this is only a guess that you arrived at by looking at one of the possible differences between cities and small towns. If you find that people in Hanover perceive that Hanover's water pollution is an important issue, your assumption was either inaccurate or, Hanover might be different from other small towns."

"But I have to find something good."

"Okay then, can you tell me what might make Hanover different from other small towns?"

After hours and hours of this torturous process, we developed three usable starting points for the project. We guessed or hypothesized that:

Residents of a small town would not perceive a water pollution problem as being a major concern either for the nation or their local community unless conditions were considered critical.

If residents of small towns perceived water pollution as a problem, they would not have a high interest in spending time addressing the problem.

Alternatively, if the first two hypotheses were falsified, then a person's perception of the water pollution problem and the intensity of their willingness to do something about it would be associated with his or her social class position as measured by occupation and level of income.

I was overjoyed when I realized that conducting research was very similar to the steps for making a peanut butter and jelly sandwich in the English class assignment: be very meticulous and precise. Because I'd never written a survey before nor had any idea how to start, Mr. Daley helped me. We wrote a broad outline of the survey and then fleshed it out with more details:

A very brief explanation of who is conducting the survey, what it is about, and assuring respondents that their replies were confidential

Demographic characteristics such as gender, age, income, occupation, level of education, and religious preference

National and local views on water pollution

Causes of water pollution

Responsibilities for water pollution

What the respondent was willing to do about water pollution

After I wrote the 20 survey questions, I still needed to figure out how to get people to complete it. Mr. Daley said there were several ways to do this, but the most important thing was to get a sample that best represented the population of Hanover so I could make generalizable conclusions about attitudes on water pollution from the research findings. He said, "You could use names from the telephone directory, but some people don't have a telephone, and married people usually have only one entry in the directory. This is usually the husband's name, so many women would be excluded. It would be better to select a representative sample from the latest voter registration list. It is a more inclusive list than the telephone directory although, of course, not everyone is registered to vote."

I asked, "How do I get one of those?"

"Go over to the Town Hall, explain to the town clerk who you are and what you're doing, and ask if you can have a voter registration list."

When I went to Town Hall, I did just that, and the town clerk mimeographed a copy of the current list of registered voters, although he insisted that I shred the list after I drew the sample. I assured him I would and returned to school as fast as I could.

The list included 1,735 names and I figured that I needed between 57 and 60 responses. I decided to select 75 potential respondents because Mr. Daley had said I should select a higher number of people to interview than was needed because some might refuse to be interviewed and others might not be available. To determine the 75 people to interview, I divided the number of people on the list by 75, used the first number on a list of random numbers to get the first name, and then took every 35th name thereafter. The strategy was to go to each person's address and ask the resident my questions. In the end, Mr. Daley was right. I was only able to interview 53 people. Of the ones I couldn't interview, five had died, ten had moved, and I couldn't find the addresses for seven.

During study halls, lunch periods, Mr. Daley's class, and occasionally after school, I went to the houses on my list and asked if the resident would be willing to participate in a survey. I informed those who agreed that,

The questionnaire is an important part of a study that I, Henry Silvert, a senior at Hanover High School, am conducting concerning the community's attitude toward certain current local issues. It shouldn't take more than ten minutes to complete. Your answers will be held in the strictest confidence. Thank you for your cooperation.

Nobody refused to be interviewed. It took me two weeks to obtain results from the 53 respondents. I learned that people in Hanover didn't conform to my perception of small towns. They *did* think that water pollution was a problem at both the national and local levels. To gauge the concern about the problem at the national level, 87 percent of the respondents agreed with the statement,

It has often been said that in the United States, we take it for granted that with a flick of the tap that we will always get clear, clean running water at any time of day, however, some experts are saying that the population explosion, sewage disposal, and industry wastes are making water pollution one of the major problems confronting our country.

Two-thirds agreed that it was also a problem in Hanover. My initial guess that people in Hanover would not be highly motivated to work to ameliorate water pollution was also inaccurate. Between 40 and 50 percent of the respondents were willing to spend time, donate money, vote on amendments, sign petitions, or support legislation to remedy the problem. While both findings contradicted my guess that Tom Lehrer's song about pollution only applied to large U.S. cities, it didn't satisfy my quest to determine which groups were likely to be among the 40 to 50 percent who would spend their resources to combat the problem.

I found that a person's perception and willingness to do something was based on different occupational categories and income levels. Public school teachers and college professors tended to have an increased perception of the problem and were more likely to spend their resources to combat it than people in other professions. People with lower levels of disposable income were less likely to perceive a national or local water pollution problem and were less prone to spend money or other resources to lessen its effects than those higher on the income ladder. This was the first of many surveys of my career, for, prior to my retirement in 2019, I spent 23 years at the Conference Board developing them and analyzing the response data. The Conference Board is a not-for-profit global, independent business membership organization and research organization working in the public interest.

* * *

THE LEAGUE OF WOMEN VOTERS

Once I'd finished writing my findings, I eagerly told one of my mother's friends, Michelle Young, about them when she was visiting one day. She stopped my spiel mid-sentence and suggested that I might like to speak with her group that Saturday because they would be discussing local efforts for cleaner water. She was the chairwoman of the local chapter of the League of

Women Voters, and they were planning to meet for about two hours in Etna, a suburb of Hanover.

Except for school presentations and my political canvassing, I was a complete novice at public speaking, though I knew I'd do a good job considering the many times I'd defended my position with my parents and teachers. When we arrived at the meeting, which was held in the basement of a church, I noticed a table with a large coffee urn, cakes, and cookies in one corner and a circle of chairs in the middle of the room. I was starting to get a little nervous, so decided to forgo loading up with coffee and sweets and went over my notes before the meeting began. All in all, there were 24 people at the meeting. Michelle called the meeting to order and, after the minutes from the previous meeting were read and accepted, she said, "As I have told most of you by phone already, Hank Silvert has just finished conducting a high school research project concerning attitudes toward water pollution in Hanover and has agreed to share some of the results with us. He will lead us in a discussion on how we can start our campaign to clean up the Connecticut River. Hank, you're on."

I didn't have any idea that I was going to be leading the discussion, but so be it. "Thank you, Michelle. I am getting a little nervous."

The woman sitting next to Michelle said, "Relax, we're an easy crowd to please."

I went on to describe my hypotheses, the survey methodology, and my findings. Before ending, I said, "Because I took a random sample, the findings reflect the attitudes of people in Hanover rather than simply the views of those who were sampled. Thus, we can say that nine out of ten people in Hanover think that water pollution is a major issue in the country, and about two-thirds also see it as a problem in Hanover. Overall, slightly fewer people than this are willing to make an effort to do something about the problem. It is interesting that people with a higher level of disposable income are much more willing to spend their time and resources on efforts against water pollution. This finding may help you in designing your outreach efforts. Thank you."

I could tell by looking at everyones' faces that I had done well. I then said, "I have never in my life led a discussion, so, Michelle or someone else can do that."

A woman sitting on the other side of the circle facing me said, "No, you're doing fine. What I am interested in is how our campaign can use your finding that income levels affect a person's willingness to address the issues related to water pollution."

This question started an intense discussion, which lasted much longer than the two hours initially allotted. By the end, there was no coffee left in the urn or sweets on the table. My parents hadn't gone to bed when I got home, so I told them everything that had happened. I had fun and learned a lot from my first foray into social science research. Mr. Daley was all smiles when I told him about my presentation at the meeting.

* * *

THE END OF A LONG QUEST

Graduation arrived in June 1967. Although my parents were ecstatic and had invited my grandmother, Dora, I thought the ceremony was anticlimactic. When I came so close to dying, neither of my parents thought I would ever graduate. On the other hand, I never doubted it. Instead of joy though, I felt both fear and anger. Fear of the unknown and of not being able to live up to my own or anyone else's expectations. Also fear of losing the few cherished friends that I had made and having to make new friends at college. I was angry that I had to leave the Hanover/Norwich communities, which had finally made me feel welcome. But most of all, I was angry because I couldn't relive that first kiss and I thought I would never have a chance at another one.

Some of us didn't approve of the main graduation speaker, a minister whose speech was laden with references to religion. We silently stood during his presentation in protest. We then moved our tassels from one side to the other to show that we had graduated. My mother and father weren't pleased either, but they behaved, although I did see my grandmother start to stand as if she were planning an attack on the speaker. My mother sprang into action, grabbing her mother and leading her out of the hall. My grandmother's actions were not unexpected, since she never hid her emotions about things she did not agree with or disliked.

Something happened to me after the ceremony concluded. When the graduating class was in line outside the hall being congratulated by the parents and other relatives, I started to cry uncontrollably. I didn't want to leave high school, and, amazingly, I didn't want to leave Hanover.

My Grandmother and Me After Graduation.

✶ ✶ ✶

LOOKING BACK

After graduation, I didn't see any of my high school classmates until our first reunion in 1987, twenty years after we graduated. Although I had mixed feelings about attending, I was curious to find out what had happened to some of them since graduation, especially those who had done their best to torture me along the way. Leading up to the reunion, I was plagued by nightmares about how I might be treated once there. In one recurring dream, a state trooper, who just happened to resemble one of the kids who called me a *right-wing, communist, fascist, pinko, bastard* and ridiculed me because I was Jewish, stopped me on the highway. In the dream, the state trooper put handcuffs on my wrists and said that, because I was driving five miles over the speed limit, he was taking me to the state penitentiary, but I woke up before he could do this.

The student in my dream didn't attend the twentieth reunion. He did attend a later one and turned out to be a very nice person who taught mathematics at a high school in New Hampshire. People can grow out of their ignorance. There had been no need for me to worry about seeing and talking to my high school buddies. In fact, my wife Morrie and I have continued to go to my class reunions every five years. I think very highly of the Hanover High School Class of 1967.

* * *

INDEPENDENCE!

I was both very excited and fearful to be going to undergraduate school in New York City. I was going to do my undergraduate studies at the University Heights campus of New York University (NYU) in the Bronx. I hoped I wouldn't experience ostracism from the teachers and students as I had when I started school at Hanover High. I worried, however, because there was always the possibility that I would be shunned.

City life excited me because of the fond memories I had of living in many cosmopolitan cities in Latin America. Yet, I had never lived in New York City, and many of my friends in Hanover and Norwich had told me that the city was very dangerous. I knew that these people rarely if ever visited the city, so I didn't believe them, but their admonitions stuck in the back of my mind. They warned me not to walk outside after four in the afternoon and, never, under any conditions, to take the subway after five. As soon as I arrived in the city my experience completely contradicted these warnings.

I was also anxious because, except for summer vacations in Mexico and Europe, I'd never lived away from my family or with a roommate, especially someone I had never met. What would I do if I didn't like my roommate? I didn't know anybody in New York City, but hoped it wouldn't be too difficult to meet people. I hoped that I'd be able to find Civil Rights and anti-war groups to join. I wondered what my classes would be like and whether I could do well enough to be able to continue onto graduate school, since my ultimate goal was to follow in my father's footsteps.

All of these issues and worries were simmering in my mind before my family and I arrived in the city in August 1967. Whenever I needed reassurance, I took comfort in my belief that I would be able to handle whatever situation arose because I had built the invisible circular wall around me long ago that I knew would always protect me. I had used this imaginary wall as a way to protect me from all those naysayers throughout my life who underestimated my abilities.

My parents were even more concerned than me about my ability to take on the academic challenges I was going to face and wondered whether they should seek professional advice. This was the first time in my life that my parents were keen on listening to professional advice from others about my education. It was a revelation to me. They had sought advice before but had often disagreed and discarded it. I wondered why they would seek advice more often from other professionals, since they were professionals themselves. What I didn't realize was that neither of my parents were specialists in the area of expertise they sought.

My mother thought that her former college roommate, Ruth Ochroch, who was now a prominent child psychologist in New York, might be able to provide some insights as to how I could adjust to the rigors of college life. We set up an appointment with her on the Monday after the whole family had relocated to the city that summer. I don't know for certain why they felt the need to move to the city where I was to attend college. Perhaps they thought I might need protection from the pressures in New York. I am sure, however, that they were somewhat relieved to be leaving Hanover, where they had never completely adapted to rural, albeit academic, life.

My father had accepted a tenured position in the Politics Department and directorship of the Latin American Studies Center at NYU's West Village Washington Square campus. He was also set to start as Latin American Social Science Adviser at the Ford Foundation, where he had been a consultant during his time at Dartmouth College. My mother was going to teach in the

Sociology Department at the City College of New York (CCNY) on Convent Avenue in Harlem, which was part of the city university system (CUNY). Benjie attended The Downtown Community School for a year before being accepted to Bronx High School of Science, and Ali would be going to City and Country School in Manhattan, before ultimately graduating from Manhattan's Friends Seminary.

After my mother introduced us, Ruth took me into the small office kitchenette, poured us coffee and put some biscuits on a plate. We discussed how I felt about moving to the city and whether I had any worries about attending college. I said I expected to like city life a lot because of all there would be to do, and I was looking forward to my upcoming adventure at college. However, I noted my fears about not being accepted because of my physical challenges. I hoped that it would all work out well and shared my discomfort about not knowing what to expect. She told me that I would always be able to call home if I felt the need or could hop onto a subway and visit my family.

Ruth specifically wanted to see how well I would handle the intellectual pressures of college life. She administered many of the same standardized tests that I had taken in high school in the more relaxed atmosphere of her office. She gave me both the English and mathematics parts of the SAT and the history and social science achievement tests. She also wanted to see how I'd do on the politics Graduate Record Exam (the GRE), despite not having started undergraduate classes. After dinner, she gave me a Rorschach test. We were done by eight o'clock.

Wow! It had been a long and intensive day. I scored higher on all the tests than I had in high school, and Ruth thought I would do well in college. She added that the Rorschach test indicated I was scared of women and she wondered why. I didn't know why, but I was quite disturbed by this finding. I did feel a little better after my mother remarked, "What teenage boy wouldn't be afraid of women?" In an interesting twist, Ruth and her husband Ed introduced me to my wife Morrie many years later. (See section "Morrie: Falling in Love" to see how Morrie and I met.)

On Wednesday of the first week in September 1967, my parents drove me to the Silver Towers, one of the two coed dorms on campus. I brought two suitcases, a typewriter, some books, a poster of Che Guevara, and snacks. My roommate hadn't arrived yet, so, after my parents left, I went out to explore. In contrast to NYU's Washington Square campus, where university buildings and dormitories neighbored other businesses, theaters, and restaurants, the University Heights campus was separated from its surrounding neighborhood by a fence. I felt like I had been transported back to a small town, except in the middle of a huge city.

While I strolled the campus, I wondered how I would get along with my roommate. I had already formed a picture of him in my mind from the letter that the NYU's admissions office sent during the summer, informing me that I would be living with Keith Secular from New Rochelle, New York. I had no idea where that was, so I looked up New Rochelle on a map and discovered it was a suburb just north of New York City in Westchester County. Since it was a suburb, I immediately thought of Levittown in Pete Seeger's rendition of *Little Boxes*. Based on this slight information, I pictured myself walking into the dorm room and finding him lying in bed wearing polka-dot pajamas and horn-rim glasses, reading the *New York Times*. I was guilty of stereotyping! After my leisurely jaunt around the campus, I returned to the room and finally met Keith. To my surprise, he was exactly who I thought he would be, down to his clothes, horn-rim glasses, and the *New York Times*. He later confessed to me that he didn't expect that I would be on the chubby side. After finding out that I lived in Norwich, Vermont, he had pictured me as tall, blond, not Jewish, and walking into the dorm room with skis. I found his stereotype somewhat hilarious. I told him that I was Jewish and asked why he hadn't thought I was Jewish in his preview of me. He said that he didn't know that there were any Jews living in Vermont. I assured him that there were only a few that I knew about and asked him whether he was Jewish. He looked at me somewhat incredulously and said, "Of course, I am." Later, I found out that, at that time, a very high percentage, somewhere between 75 and 80 percent, of NYU students were Jewish.

Keith and I continued to be roommates both on and off campus until we graduated in 1971, with the exception of his junior year, which he spent at the London School of Economics.

* * *

EXCITING ACTIVISM
AND ANEMIC ACADEMICS

Academically speaking, my first year at college was not one of my best. I was plagued by the same problems that had hampered me throughout most of my high school years, including an inability to remember details when they weren't presented in a contextual framework. This prevented me from doing well on multiple-choice tests and other classroom exercises. To me, introductory level courses were only about memorizing facts, reading dull textbooks, and meeting unreasonable demands. Many of the classes had so many students and so little student participation that they ended up feeling impersonal. My introduction to sociology class, for example, had about a hundred students, which made it difficult for any extensive discussion. In addition, the final exam consisted of 150 true/false questions, 200 positive multiple-choice questions (selecting the correct answer), and 250 negative multiple-choice questions (selecting the incorrect answer). Of course, I did miserably on the test, only getting ten answers correct, a statistically significant high number of incorrect responses. I was elated when the professor offered me the chance to retake the test in his office and write a response to an essay question. I never took another course with him because I worried that I would be given another exam like that one.

My freshman English class was nearly as disastrous as sociology. Both the midterm and the final exams were a combination of short answer and essay questions. What saved me was an assignment to write a "creative" story. I was stumped: what would constitute a creative story? Somewhere, in the depth of my consciousness, I had a feeling that the professor wanted us to think about writing about something out of the ordinary because she always provided tidbits about the authors we were studying that seemed to have nothing to do with their writings. But this insight didn't help me determine the content of my creative story. I was still having trouble figuring out a theme or plot on the afternoon before the assignment was due when I had a discussion about cafeteria food with four friends in my dorm room. I started to frantically write down the exchange, including notes about the levels and cadence of the voices as they changed and other mannerisms. I used all of this information for a one-act play. Each of the characters was assigned a different ethnicity, but the ethnicity was assigned its derogatory name in the listing of characters. The play received the highest grade in the class and the professor read it to the class.

I was looking forward to my political science classes, as these would be my specialty. However, I thought that the textbook in my Introduction to Politics class was rather mundane because it spent 300 or so pages arguing that politics is talk. This thesis seemed overly simplistic given the social inequality at home and the planes dropping missiles in Vietnam.

Compared to Hanover High School, there was a large group of students who were involved in the anti-war movement. For the first time in my life, I felt a kinship with my peers, even if none of them were friends yet and I did not know much about their political views except that they believed as I did about the war. Two months after starting college, I joined a group of students headed downtown to join an anti-war/anti-military draft demonstration in front of the draft center in Lower Manhattan. This protest was the largest anti-war protest I had ever attended.

There must have been thousands of people already assembled when we arrived. I started helping a woman who was passing out flowers and peace buttons. I don't know how it happened, but we suddenly found ourselves surrounded by police mounted on horses and were almost kicked by one of the horses as it reared up on its hind legs. We escaped without anything unfortunate happening. Instead of leaving, we decided to rejoin the others in the demonstration.

I was fascinated to learn that aside from protesting against the U.S. involvement in Vietnam, there had been almost a decade of protests on college campuses around the country and the world concerning freedom of speech within the academic community. These included a focus on Civil Rights, and expectations of university members regarding their responsibility to their surrounding communities. While I'd been somewhat aware about the activities of other activists, it wasn't until I arrived in New York that I realized the profound impact students were having through political organizing and protesting both on and off university and college campuses. They were speaking out on issues identical to those about which I was interested and becoming more passionate. I found out, for example, that as early as 1964, students in the Free Speech Movement at the Berkeley Campus of the University of California organized and were victorious in their efforts to obtain the right to participate in political activities on and near the college campus.

Only a couple of months had elapsed when I grudgingly realized that my anti-war and Civil Rights work had to take second place to academics, or I'd be forced to leave the university. I almost flunked out in my first semester. Although I continued to find most of my classes boring, I began to attend them with the sole purpose of obtaining reasonable grades. To have more time for my studies, I stopped playing bridge in the dorm lounge, although I continued to play at the college bridge club.

The only class I took that semester that I didn't find boring was Political Theory. Its syllabus consisted of the very same books that I had read and discussed with my father during my high school summers, including those by Machiavelli, Hobbes, Locke, Rousseau, and Marx. What was different was that, for the first time, I'd be discussing these works with people who did not always agree with my interpretation. The professor and most of the students seemed to be enamored with versions of the more violent Hobbesian or Lockean social contract models rather than my preference for the more communitarian nature of society presented by Rousseau or Marx. Nevertheless, I relished the give and take of the classroom discussions. What I found utterly irritating, however, was the narrow mindedness of the final take-home exam, which the professor said could be no longer than three typewritten pages. None of us took him literally, but we should have. No matter the quality of the essay, he took half a letter grade off for each word over the three-page limit. I received a D+ because I went nine words into the fourth page. This was higher than the class average, which was a D. I still consider the essay to be one of the best papers I've ever written.

One of my weirdest experiences during this period was when someone stole my shoes during swim class. When I arrived at the dorm barefoot, Keith had a big chuckle about what had happened. When he offered to loan me a pair of his so I could buy some new shoes, we discovered that we wore the same size. It was just another of the many surprising things we had in common.

* * *

THE GORDON AFFAIR

My second semester English class syllabus consisted of books written by late 18th century and 19th century English writers. Our professor, Nicholas Gordon, focused on the intersection between the subject matter of the books and the social, economic, and political changes of their time. Through this analysis, I was finally able to understand how literature, or at least some of it, reflected current events in society. I wrote a lengthy essay connecting the literature of the day to the Industrial Revolution and the emergence of a vibrant bourgeoisie as exemplified by the French Revolution of 1848. On our final exam, I wrote the shortest answer to an essay question that I have ever written and, in spite of this, received a high grade. It was one semi-long paragraph. This was the kind of engaging class that I needed. I felt so comfortable in Mr. Gordon's class that as he passed me on the campus green one evening, I greeted him by saying, "Hi, Nick."

He responded, "Hi, Hank."

When I realized what I'd done, I stopped dead in my tracks and said, "Oh, I'm sorry, Professor Gordon, I didn't mean to call you by your first name."

He said, "Oh, that's alright. Did you hear the terrible news? Martin Luther King, Jr. was assassinated."

"Oh, no I didn't."

This was devastating news, and I rushed back to the dorm to find many of the students huddled around a television in the lobby watching news of the assassination.

I was still processing this loss two days later when students learned that the English Department had not offered Professor Gordon a tenured position for the following year, which meant he would have to leave the university at the end of the semester. We found out the department's official reason for not giving him tenure was that he had not published a sufficient number of articles in academic journals or books or contributed to the university's community outreach efforts. While these were legitimate reasons, we also learned that the university had weighed rumors that he was one of the editors of the communist newspaper the *Daily Worker,* had participated in the poor people's campaign in Washington D.C., and that he was gay. These factors, we thought, were not grounds for tenure refusal.

What could we do to find out the "true" reason that he was denied tenure and voice our strong disapproval of this action? We developed a two-pronged approach during our strategy meetings, although we didn't have much faith that either would impact the decision. The first was simply to approach the English Department chair about the department's actions and request a town hall style meeting to discuss them with students. The second step was to circulate a petition asking the administration to reconsider its decision.

The English Department and the university's administration didn't approve of either of these approaches on the grounds that academic freedom would be stifled. On the contrary, we thought that an open dialogue was essential to academic freedom, and transparency would enhance wider student participation in the process. What was to be done, now? After a couple of weeks and what seemed like an endless series of meetings, we decided that the only means left to express our displeasure was to have a nonviolent sit-in in a building essential to the university's functioning. We decided to occupy the building that housed the campus provost's office.

Early one morning, about 100 of us went into the building and sat down on the main stairwell leading to the classrooms and offices. During the day, many more students joined us. There were no elevators in the building, however people could access the upper floors using the fire exit stairs in the back of the building. In reality, we made it only slightly inconvenient for those who needed to attend classes or who worked in the administrative offices. The campus police initially accused us of violating a building code by blocking the main stairwell but left us alone when we pointed out that we weren't completely blocking access.

Our efforts to save Professor Gordon's job failed, and he didn't return to teach the following semester. Although we fell short of achieving our primary goal, the process we used to plan the protest taught me a vital lesson. When planning any protest, it is best to start at a very simplistic, non-confrontational level in order to build support, and then increase pressure in incremental steps. In the case of the struggle to save Professor Gordon's job, we began with a petition and built up to the sit-in, which broadened support for the protest to many liberal arts and engineering students who were not initially concerned about the issue.

* * *

OTHER CAUSES, OTHER PROTESTS

While we deeply believed in our protests to save Professor Gordon's job, our struggles seemed minor compared to those taking place at several other universities in the New York City area. At the City College of New York (CCNY), students were organizing about affirmative action issues. At Columbia University, the Student Afro-American Society (SAS) and the Students for a Democratic Society (SDS) were building a coalition to stop the university's eviction of Harlem residents to build a gymnasium as well as to cut the institution's ties to the government administration's war efforts in Vietnam. These efforts culminated with the student takeover of the Columbia University campus on April 28, 1968.

Issues related to race also roiled our campus. Within months after the assassination of Dr. Martin Luther King Jr., our university, like many other universities and colleges around the country, established an African American

Studies Center, which was located at the Washington Square campus. Shortly after a director for the center was hired, he was fired without any reason. Rumors about the firing were legion, ranging from his conflicts with the university's administration and faculty to his anti-Semitic statements and sentiments. His firing enraged two groups of students in NYU's University Heights campus in different ways. Members of Katara (the African American organization at the Bronx campus) insisted that he had not been provided due legal process and called for his reinstatement until this was in place.

The SDS, on the other hand, argued that his firing was simply a bourgeois hoax that enabled the established powers and ruling elite to get rid of a rabble-rouser. My interpretation of the differences between the two groups' reasoning was that Katara's argument was procedural, whereas the SDS's stemmed from an ideological stance. From my point of view, it seemed like Katara was framing its position much along the lines that I had learned to be most effective during the protests about the Gordon affair.

After a long joint meeting, including passionate and sometimes loud position statements in support of each group's position, it became evident that their differences were irreconcilable. Late that night, Katara and the SDS reached an agreement that the next day Katara would have a sit-in at the student center and the SDS would sit-in at the library. I had no intention of sitting-in at the library with the SDS. I wanted to join Katara's protest at the student center because I thought their position was more tenable. However, the time was not ripe for me to participate. Katara wished to show solidarity with the African American students. The protest was taking place during a time of increased African American identity and empowerment and the emergence of "Black Is Beautiful." Therefore, in consultation with the African American students, I decided not to enter the student union. They suggested that if I didn't want to go to the library with the SDS, I should stay at the campus entrance. I think that because of Katara's position that African American solidarity was necessary, there was widespread support among a majority of students of all races and ethnicities that there should be due process and an open discussion concerning the reasons for the director's dismissal. But, of course, the university administration refused to discuss its decisions with us because, as with Professor Gordon, it would infringe on their academic freedom.

The day of the sit-ins was tense. On one side of the green, only members of Katara could enter the student center, while, on the other side of the green, the library was closed to everyone except members of the SDS. The sit-in at the library probably infuriated the administration most because it blocked access to one of the university's treasures, a walkway overlooking the East River and upper Manhattan. Students who didn't want to be part of either demonstration but supported the protest sat cross-legged at the campus gates to prevent cars from entering. NYU's administration had requested protection from the New York Police Department (NYPD), so there was a ring of policemen (no women) on the outside of the fence surrounding the campus at attention with guns in their holsters and batons at the ready in their hands.

I was not going to sit down and block cars, although I thought it was a good idea, I just felt that there must be a more active approach I could take. What was I to do? I decided to try a little experiment. What would the police do if I just went up and started conversations with them? I started talking with one policeman outside of the main campus entrance and then continued on to the next telling them why we were sitting-in, asking why they were supporting an unjust decision, and suggesting that they lay down their guns and join us. None of them said a word to me, and none of them put down their guns and joined us. They just stared at me or straight ahead. Although this exercise took all day, it was fun and exhausting, and I had done something for the cause.

As with our efforts to reinstate Professor Gordon, our protest was ultimately unsuccessful. Still, it was a learning experience. If politics is talk, as my textbook claimed, it became clear the administration of the university wasn't interested in having a conversation with its students.

* * *

CHOOSING MY PATH

When Keith took his junior year abroad, I moved out of the dorm with two other students into a six-room apartment on the top floor of a two-story house near the corner of West Tremont and Grand Avenue, about a 15-minute walk from campus. The walls needed plastering, and the entire apartment needed painting, as well as other major repairs. Before classes started in August, we went to work on the apartment. When it came time to paint the rooms, we could not agree on the colors. We finally decided on light blue for the living room, the kitchen, and the bathroom. Each of us was left to decide which color to paint our own rooms. I decided to paint my room a dark purple and the molding a modest, light, shade of orange. I thought it prudent to get permission from our landlady before putting my design in place.

Her instantaneous reply was, "Do whatever the hell you want to do!"

The expletive in her response was indicative of her reaction to other things that occurred during our year there. She often saw us coming in or going out the front door and asked, using the derogatory term for Chinese, "Are you going to eat Chink food tonight?" We would always simply respond by saying, "No, we're not going to eat Chinese food tonight."

When we told her that the water from the kitchen faucet was coming out a dirty, dark brown, she said, "That only happens once in a blue moon. It will soon go away." Indeed, it inevitably did go away by itself, although it sometimes took two or three days.

Both our landlady and her daughter had full-time jobs at a company in downtown Manhattan. Despite working eight hours a day during the week, her daughter made a cake for the Mets baseball team every time they won a game. She also made a cake every time a player on the team had a birthday. Since she had season tickets to the games, she delivered her cakes in person. To their credit, neither she nor her mother ever complained about anything we did, despite our frequent loud music and parties. The vast difference in language and vocabulary between our landlady and her daughter and the three of us reminded me of the differences that I'd taken note of in Hanover between those who were associated with Dartmouth College and those who weren't.

After Keith's year studying in London, we, along with two of our close friends, Asher and Roger who had already graduated and had jobs, started looking for a place to live that was a little closer to campus. We found a large apartment on the top floor of a two-story house on Harrison Avenue between

West Tremont and Burnside Avenue, only a block closer to the campus than the apartment I'd lived in the year before. We got along very well and decided that each one of us would make dinner every fourth night. My favorite dishes to cook were sweet-and-sour pork, or hamburger or chicken *a la Hank*. I didn't exactly know the recipe for sweet and sour sauce, but the concoction I made consisted of ketchup, mustard, canned pineapple chunks and the juice, and I added whatever main ingredient was available that night. For dessert, I always served a dozen donuts and coffee. Sometimes, I'd go to Mr. Green's butcher shop on the corner and ask him to prepare a delicious meal for us. He always knew exactly what I meant and most of the time put together a meat loaf that we only had to reheat.

While I knew that I'd eventually major in politics, I checked out other courses as well. Always in my mind was a desire to emulate my father, who, though his principal area of concentration was political science, was quite knowledgeable in other subjects as well. I also calculated that since the politics major only required 24 credits, I could take one 3-credit politics course for eight semesters and satisfy the requirement. So, I did not declare the major until the beginning of my junior year. I decided to minor in Spanish, but, in the end, I had enough credits to have also minored in sociology as well as philosophy.

My sophomore year brought a change in the way I thought and approached college. I expanded my circle of friends and started enjoying my classes more. The most memorable class was one offered by the Sociology Department called Scientific Research Methods. It reminded me of my twelfth grade Science and Issues class, although the professor was not as adept as the teacher I'd had in high school. The instructor walked in on the first day of class, plopped her bags on her desk, and, without introducing herself, proclaimed, "You can't predict human behavior because everyone has freewill. Are there any questions?"

I couldn't believe this was how she began the class, especially after the research I'd conducted on water pollution. I asked, "What are we doing here if not trying to predict human behavior?"

She said, "I just don't believe that we can predict human behavior." Then, she proceeded to hand out the course syllabus and tell us about the class requirements and, although this wasn't an auspicious start, the class rapidly improved, despite the instructor's approach.

Later in the semester, the professor subdivided the class into groups to work on a project, which included writing and distributing a survey and analyzing its results. I was in the largest group, which also turned out to be the most ambitious. While the other groups developed their research problem and hypotheses around how students chose a major or decided what classes to take, we asked ourselves why some people stole from the college bookstore. *Our major hypothesis was that people stole books because they felt alienated from their class work.* In addition to class time, we spent two weeks researching the literature on the issue and writing a ten-page research proposal.

When we handed it in, we expected it would be approved immediately, but that wasn't the case. After reviewing our proposal, the professor's first comment was, "There is no theft from the bookstore. It's not possible to steal from there. You'll have to find another project."

We were shocked into silence for a moment, but then someone suggested that she accompany us and sit outside the college bookstore, and we would show her that not only was it possible to steal from the bookstore but that we could do so without being caught. I never had stolen anything from the bookstore, but I knew of others who had. We managed to prevail upon her to join us after class. At the bookstore, we asked her to sit in a chair just outside while we went inside to shoplift some books. When we came out with our stash, she was both shocked and convinced that theft was an issue but then told us to return the books. Of course, we couldn't do this because we'd be arrested. Grudgingly she approved our project, and we proceeded to write our survey and ask students to complete it as they left the bookstore.

We were able to confirm our hypothesis by tabulating the results and running them through a card sorter, just as I had done in high school. We found that students who stole from the bookstore were more likely than those who didn't steal to think that their classes did nothing to enhance their education and were not worthy of their time.

The Foreign Policy class that I took with Professor James Crown was the most memorable political science course during my four undergraduate years. He reinforced the importance of geography that I had only tangentially addressed in high school when I traced maps of countries highlighting their cities, rivers, and mountain ranges. Now, Professor Crown asked us to examine Southeast Asia's topography and its impact on the Vietnam civil war. I was aided in this process by remembering *The Ugly American*.

My two favorite classes junior year were Political Philosophy and Latin American Political Theory. The Latin American theory class was a graduate class given at NYU's Washington Square campus by Professor Pedro Cuperman, from Argentina. He concentrated on different understandings of development, modernization, and dependency in Latin America, all of which I'd heard discussed at home but had never before read anything about. Because the professor's English was not great, and his Spanish accent was still strong, throughout the class sessions other students would pass me notes asking me to clarify what he was saying. A particularly difficult word for him to say was legitimacy, which he would pronounce as "elegetemacy".

I also found my Philosophy class, which concentrated on Greek and Medieval philosophers, vastly entertaining and informative. I loved the reading assignments, from writings by Plato to Machiavelli, and relished participating in classroom discussions and writing the required essays. The professor, Harold McClendon, was one of my favorites with his strange yet somewhat empowering classroom demeanor. The first time he walked into class, he said, "We are not going to have class this Thursday because of Rosh Hashanah. Does anyone disagree?" All of us shook our heads, *no*. The next Monday, he walked into class and stated, "We are not going to have class this Thursday because of Yom Kippur. Does anyone disagree?" Again, no one objected (although there are ten days between Rosh Hashanah and Yom Kippur).

Since a large majority of students at NYU were Jewish, these two cancelations seemed only natural. The third Monday of the semester, Professor McClendon walked in and once again said, "We won't be having classes this Thursday. Does anyone disagree?" I raised my hand and asked what the reason was this time, and he responded, "I just don't want to hold classes on Thursdays." From then on, we never had classes on Thursdays.

He also gave us the option of working for either an A or B in the class, which required students to take tests and write a paper, or just to get a C, which required no work at all. I was the only one not to request the opportunity for an A or B. I was surprised to find that I received an A for the class. Later that year, I asked him why he had not followed through with my grade? He told me that since I had done all the work, he couldn't give me a C.

That semester I served as an Alternate Student Representative on the Curriculum Committee, and Professor McClendon was one of the faculty members on the committee. Both faculty and students on the committee advocated for students to add more required classes than those already on the books. However, I didn't think there should be any requirements. Instead, I suggested there should be an extensive faculty advisory system set up to explain to students the reason for each course the faculty member would recommend. All of those on the committee were invited to attend a general faculty meeting to discuss our conclusions and I was invited to argue my case, ultimately to no avail.

Two months later, however, all course requirements were abolished. A few days afterward I passed Professor McClendon on the green and he said, with a twinkle in his eyes, "You got your way!" Many years after I graduated, we ran into each other on the corner of Bleecker Street and LaGuardia Place. During our conversation he said, "There was a very nice professor with the same last name as yours who died last year. Was he any relation to you?"

I said, "That was my father."

He said, "Oh, I'm sorry I asked. I didn't know."

I said, "Actually, that is the nicest thing you could have asked. I don't want people to like me because I am my father's son."

HERTFORD COLLEGE, OXFORD

Just as I thought it wasn't necessary to declare a major before my junior year, I didn't think I had to start thinking about graduate schools until at least the end of the first semester of my senior year. Therefore, I was surprised the first Saturday of February in my junior year when, while visiting my family in their West Village apartment, I picked up the ringing phone and a man, with an upper-class heavily accented English voice said, "Hello, my name is Raymond Carr, can I speak to Hal?"

I said, "There is no one by that name here. You have the wrong number."

"It's the boy who wants to go to Oxford University."

"Oh, that's me. My name is Hank." Although I had no idea of how he'd gotten my name, I knew my mother and father had decided I should go to a "British finishing school" after I graduated.

"Oh, good. Could you meet me at the Horn and Hardart Bar in Penn Station at five this afternoon?"

"Sure."

I caught my father up on things when he got home and he said he'd mentioned to Raymond at a conference that I wanted to go to graduate school in England, but had no idea I'd get a call so soon.

I put on my corduroy jacket with a peace button on the lapel and took the subway to Penn Station. When I entered the bar, Dr. Carr got up to shake my hand. After seeing my button, he told me how he had joined the international brigades that fought against Francisco Franco during the Spanish Civil War. I shared what I was doing in the anti-war effort. Then we began talking about graduate school and how I might fit into life at Oxford. I said that I would like to study Latin American politics. He told me about the wonderful Latin American Center at Oxford. He was enthusiastic that Oxford University would be a good fit for me though noted that it was too late to get me into an Oxford college for the next year. In the meantime, he could get me admitted into the University of Essex and I would be able to transfer to Oxford the following year. I let him know that I had another year before completing my undergraduate studies and would not be available for graduate school until after completing my studies at NYU. We shook hands, and he left to take a taxi to the airport for his return to England.

Early in my senior year, I received an application to Oxford, which I completed and returned. The application asked that I choose the top three colleges I wanted to attend at Oxford, but I didn't know about the individual colleges so didn't select any. I never completed an application for the University of Essex and, therefore, was surprised in April when I received a letter congratulating me on my acceptance.

After graduating from NYU in June 1971, I spent the summer reading at our summer house in Norwich and swimming at Storrs Pond in Hanover. Before heading to England, I planned to spend a few days in New York in September. While going through the mail after arriving in New York, I found a surprise. There was a letter from Hertford (pronounced *Hartford*) College, Oxford, notifying me of my acceptance to the Bachelor of Philosophy (B.Phil.) in Latin American Studies and that the Michealmas (fall) term would begin on October 15. I immediately decided to attend Oxford instead of Essex and called my parents to tell them of my change in plans.

As my September 15 plane ticket from New York to London was non-refundable, I decided to drop my luggage at Hertford College, take a ferry to Gothenburg, Sweden, and then a train to see a friend who was learning Swedish at the University in Uppsala. When I returned to Hertford College, I discovered that because the college was considered an undergraduate college, it didn't provide living accommodations (digs) for its graduate students. I eventually found quarters two blocks away from Hertford College across the street from New College, which, despite its name, is one of the oldest colleges at Oxford.

My Hertford ID

I was also instructed to register at Oxford's Bodleian Library. When I arrived at the library wearing my academic gown, which all students were required to wear at formal dinners and other important events, I was asked to swear that I wouldn't bring pens into the library or deface the books in any way. They did not permit books to be taken out of the building. Instead, librarians brought the books to the reading room you were in and provided pens with erasable ink. After 14 days, a librarian would automatically return the books to the stacks. Each college, institute, and department had its own specialized library, which permitted students to check out books. I was informed that I would be a junior member of St. Antony's College, which housed the Latin American Center.

At Oxford, I wrote three six page essays a week that I read aloud and discussed with each of my tutors. I saw each tutor, who specialized in different areas of Latin America, on a one-to-one basis. I almost never finished my reading of an essay with one particular tutor because she would start a free-flowing conversation about the subject of the essay. My job was to back up my part of the conversation with facts and figures from within my paper. During the first year, I wrote an in-depth proposal for my thesis on Chile. My academic advisor had written a very detailed analysis of the emergence of workers' unions in Chile and suggested that I include a discussion of the role of labor unions in Chilean politics.

164

GRADUATE SCHOOL
BACK IN THE STATES

My visiting professorship at The Colegio de Mexico was coming to an end in September 1976, and I was searching the possibilities of teaching somewhere else in Mexico. Then early in the morning on June 5, I received a call from my mother informing me that my father had died suddenly of a heart attack. He had visited me as recently as a month prior, as he had some Ford Foundation business to do in Mexico. The last dinner we had was on his last day in the country. One of his Chilean colleagues from the foundation's Mexican office invited us for dinner at his home. When we arrived, he introduced us to his wife and, Mercedes, a Chilean friend who taught at the Autonomous University of Mexico (UNAM).

While having drinks, Mercedes began grilling my father, in Spanish of course, about how he as a Yankee from the United States could understand anything about Latin America. I could just see my father's anger rise as he began explaining the extensive work he had done in the region. During dinner, this friend talked about the unrest at the university where she taught and ended by saying, "What can we do when the students' demands keep pushing us to the political right? I am not a fascist."

My father turned to her and with a perfect Chilean accent, calmly said, "Well, you are a fascist." I had never heard him call someone a fascist before. I was very proud.

My father's death prompted me to reframe my immediate plans for the future. I returned to New York to be with my family. Shortly thereafter, I entered the doctoral program in sociology at NYU. It was during my time there that I fully appreciated the influence my father and mother had on me. I more fully understood their insistence to always question the wisdom and thinking of others. Based on my father's academic interactions with colleagues and students, I had a rather utopian view of life as a graduate student. I imagined my graduate studies would be a continuous exchange of ideas with colleagues, and that professors and students, while at different levels of achievement, would engage with one another as equals. My mother, who primarily taught undergraduates, treated her students as equals. While my parents' openness to dialogue was a powerful model for my own intellectual advancement, current faculty members did not always follow it. During my first months of graduate school, I formed the impression that my professors viewed themselves as the source of all insights, the kings and queens of knowledge who could never misinterpret knowledge and should never be questioned. Although my teachers' attitudes were frustrating, I was not going to let their lack of collegiality interfere with my mission not only to receive a doctorate but to learn how to combine theoretical knowledge with statistical back up.

At Oxford, I'd attended a lecture at Ruskin College, a workers' college in the city of Oxford but not part of the university. The speaker was Ernest Mandel, the Secretary General of the Trotskyist Fourth International, who astutely supported his theoretical views of the world using statistical analysis. Outside of the rudimentary survey research analysis I had conducted on water pollution and theft in the student bookstore, I was still a novice at statistical analysis. One of the main reasons I entered the doctorate program at NYU was to learn how to conduct analyses on Mandel's level. I planned to take as many statistics courses as possible so I could use what I learned to argue my theoretical views. As usual, the introduction to statistics was quite burdensome, as I had no idea why it was necessary to learn all of those formulas. I needed to immerse myself in learning statistics just as I had done with learning different languages and bridge. I had to learn the mechanics of calculating averages, medians, modes, standard deviations, and variances to appreciate both the logic behind these concepts and their usage. As typified by my style of learning, since I didn't comprehend why we were studying each of these techniques, it was difficult for me to remember the formulas for the calculations. As a result, I didn't do well in my first semester statistics course. However, I finally caught on and figured out exactly why we learned those esoteric formulas when the professor demonstrated their use during the first day of second semester statistics.

While the beginning statistics classes focused on technical issues involving memorization of formulas, the more advanced classes were practical and substantive. It was these later classes that provided insights as to the reasoning for the specific formulas to use to support my findings and explained the importance of knowing how to utilize them.

Sociology does not rest on statistical analysis alone, and my social scientific theoretical knowledge when I entered the doctoral program was largely based on global issues and, of course, my field research on Chilean social and political development. I felt statistics would enable me to amplify my theoretical interpretations. I quickly realized that most courses were centered on the United States social structure rather than considering sociology from a global perspective. I love sociological theory, but I was perplexed by the way some professors used it in an ethnocentric manner. I was especially disturbed when a professor took Max Weber's conceptualization of different forms of political legitimacy out of its original context and forced it to fit into a mold suited for this country alone. This instance of what I call "academic ethnocentrism" occurred when I audited a graduate political sociology class in the late 1970s. I didn't want to take the class for credit as I had taken the same course with the same professor as an undergraduate. The professor laid out Max Weber's three theoretical, ideal typical forms of political legitimacy, including the distinctive characteristics of each. It was then time for the class to participate in a discussion about them. One of the students, and I swear it wasn't me, raised his hand and asked in what category of legitimacy the professor would classify President Allende of Chile. This was an intriguing question as it attempted to attach a theoretical formulation to a historical event.

The professor's only comment was, "Allende's presidency was not legitimate, and he was assassinated because he did not have the support of the people." After saying he didn't "have anything else to say about the matter," he moved onto another topic, even though several students wanted to continue to discuss the topic.

As far as Weber's types of political legitimacy were concerned, I'd argue that Allende's presidency fit at least two of Weber's categories. He would definitely not fit into a traditional form of legitimacy, which would best be associated with a feudal or caste social structure. However, Allende's presidency and the Popular Unity administration could have been characterized as a charismatic form of political legitimacy, where a person's character or personality spurs the transition from one form of social structure to another. However, Chilean social and political structure was based on a bureaucratic, constitutional, social class system, which Weber classified as a rational legal form of legitimacy. A society of this nature is one that is based on law, merit, and high levels of education. In my view, if we wanted to use Weber's contribution, that would be the best way to describe Allende's presidency.

In addition to letting his political biases get in the way of a dispassionate discussion of Weber's concepts, the professor applied the concept of legitimacy in a limited sense of applying it to a specific leader rather than as a broader, general concept. What made the conversation frustrating was the professor's use of "legitimacy" as a substitute for the word "legitimate." Legitimacy refers to the way a society is structured, the way people in a society behave toward each other, not the way a particular person is viewed. Weber's conceptualization of the different types of legitimacy focused on whether they were based on ascriptive (arbitrary), feudal, or caste characteristics, autocratic leadership, or merit and social class criteria. Allende was considered a legitimate president by a plurality of Chileans, whether they were from the lower, middle, and working classes, or upper class. Obviously, not all Chileans supported him. These results supported Weber's overall point that in a rational legal framework, social class rather than caste predominates in the social structure. Don't get me wrong, this is no excuse for the toppling of a functioning democracy. I do think, however, this is a much more useful way of applying Weber's concepts to a concrete situation.

Under these adverse conditions, I knew that it would be difficult to find a dissertation topic that would be approved if it dealt with a foreign country. I wondered whether either of the topics I was considering would appeal to Juan Corradi, a sociology professor from Argentina. My first dissertation proposal was a continuation of the research on the impact of social class on conceptions of nationalism that I'd started while in Mexico. The initial results of this research had indicated that people at different levels of social class, using Weber's conceptualization that it is a combination of class, status, and power, have different perceptions of the nation-state.

The second dissertation proposal was an attempt to understand the reasons that after more than 40 years of fascism, Spain peacefully became a democratic country when Francisco Franco died. My hypothesis was that this was partially due to the role that artists and writers had played in maintaining a democratic spirit throughout the dictatorship. I thought that the horrors of Franco's fascism portrayed in paintings and novels could act as a catalyst for a return to democracy. I felt a deep connection with these topics, and spent several months writing proposals for both. As I feared, neither was accepted.

A professor who became my faculty adviser convinced me to conduct a time-series analysis on a sociological topic. In this case, although I agreed to use a statistical methodology, I was still left with a decision as to its topic. The professor suggested I examine occupational mobility using this technique. As I started to do a literature search on the issue, I learned there were many controversial points of view about the process of social mobility. After reviewing the work of so many well-known and respected scholars, I would hardly have time to add anything new to the dialogue. I thought that an alternative topic would be a time-series analysis of the social impact of energy consumption in the post-industrial United States. I was very much influenced because of OPEC's 1973 oil embargo in this country and its impact on the price of products that use oil and gasoline. My dissertation advisor and two other professors approved of this topic, although they did so somewhat grudgingly because they thought that it would be more appropriately considered a topic for the Economics Department.

I had to do lot of work to convince them that this topic was indeed a sociological one. It helped my cause that a ferocious energy debate had been brewing since the embargo. Although energy and other business executives were concerned about the impact of energy consumption on society and the environment, there was little sociological research on the issue. I felt that the controversies between three major perspectives in the debate could easily be used as hypotheses in my research. Each presented a different way of understanding the social and economic impact of increasing use of nonrenewable energy sources on the process of industrialization. I also greatly appreciated that there was extremely little sociological literature on the debate as this presented the possibility that I could contribute a new understanding of the subject and the literature review would be manageable.

The expansionist view—the most widely held perspective—argued that as energy consumption increases, so does the quality of life. The decoupling view held that the expansionists were accurate in their historical assessment, but that there was a disassociation between energy use and other economic and social well-being in advanced stages of industrialization. The third perspective, the sociocultural perspective, maintained that when energy consumption increases, this results in a negative impact on the quality of life.

After research of the available data, I found yearly time series stretching back to 1929 on energy consumption, per capital gross domestic product, the unemployment rate, wholesale prices, life expectancy, death rates, suicide rates, and divorce rates, which roughly coincided with the beginning of the Great Depression. There were no time series going back to 1850 that covered the entire period of industrialization, so I had to use findings from other researchers and sources.

My research focused on the primary reason I had originally entered the doctoral program: to determine whether it was possible to use a statistical platform to support a theoretical understanding of social change. My hunch, or hypothesis in social scientific lingo, from a literature review, was that the decoupling view in the energy debate would more likely reflect social changes in the United States. I found that historical context matters. Increased use of consumer products was very closely tied to increases in energy consumption before the 1920s. However, this relationship decreased as consumption of coal and wood was replaced by oil and gas, which in turn was replaced by electricity, a secondary form of energy consumption. I proposed that, at least for the United States, the decoupling argument suggests that it would be possible to decrease consumption of nonrenewable energy sources while finding more advantageous ways of using renewable sources such as solar energy.

When I arrived 30 minutes before my dissertation oral defense, my adviser, Richard Maisel, called me to his office. He said, "Don't get upset if

Dennis or Juan suggest that you write it over and insert a theoretical argument." It was then, that I knew that he had never read the dissertation, and that his sole concern was my chapter on the methodological framework. I had asked Dennis Wrong and Juan Coradi, to be on the committee because I knew that, although we had different views of the world, they would not let it influence them. After I introduced myself and summarized my findings, Dennis began, "Hank, this is one of the best theses I have ever read, but before you submit it, please check for spelling mistakes. I'm sure it was a typo, but you misspelled an author's name in the bibliography." I could see my adviser slouch down in his seat and give a sigh of relief. Dennis, Richard, my wife, and I then went out for lunch at an Italian restaurant on MacDougal Street. I was honored that day to receive my doctorate, and I just had to fix a typo rather than completely revise my dissertation.

My NYU graduation

MY PARENTS' SON

Because of my parents' interest in politics, I naturally sought political solutions to the prejudice and discrimination I faced in New Orleans and Hanover. I thought the answers I searched for could be found by working in the Civil Rights and anti-war movements. As I became aware that the Vietnamese conflict wasn't going to end before I graduated from high school, I faced the remote possibility that I would be drafted. (In the end, I had to go for a military draft physical.) Although I didn't know it at the time, I understood later that my political activism and awareness was an important part of my education.

* * *

ACTIVISM: CIVIL RIGHTS WORK

Although there have always been extreme pockets of animosity, dislike, and jealousy between peoples of different nations, I felt there must be a way to ameliorate, if not eliminate these feelings once and for all. I thought I could help by getting involved with efforts in the Hanover/Norwich vicinity to assist the Civil Rights movement and anti-war efforts. I volunteered to work with the local branch of the National Association for the Advancement of Colored People (NAACP), which designated the week of May 11, 1964, as Freedom Week, to raise funds for the Mississippi Summer Project. This initiative was sponsored by a coalition including the Student Nonviolent Coordinating

Committee (SNCC), the Congress of Racial Equality (CORE), the Southern Christian Leadership Conference (SCLC), and the NAACP. The money raised during Freedom Week would be used to set up and equip schools, voter registration offices, and community centers throughout the Southern states.

Our fund-raising activities included a Civil Rights rally and art exhibits as well as auctions in Hanover and surrounding Upper Valley towns. I went to the Civil Rights rally and then sold refreshments during the Hanover art auction. The sale of sandwiches, sodas, cookies, and coffee netted $500. I was surprised that people often rounded their payments up to the next dollar rather than ask for change. It was interesting and fun to see people from all walks of life coming together to work for a single cause.

The exuberance I felt participating in these events encouraged me to push the prior bad high school experiences to the back of my mind. I was discovering, to my delight, that there were many others in the community who felt as I did about social and economic injustice and inequality. I even imagined that everyone, at least in Hanover, would join in the struggle. This was, of course, at least a bit premature or a pure fantasy since Hanover, Dartmouth College, and the surrounding towns were generally fairly conservative and not in the least thinking along the same lines as I was.

While learning about community organization and the Civil Rights movement, I felt marginalized and isolated because none of my high school buddies were involved. However, I was gratified when, in part through our organizing efforts, a contingent of Dartmouth students decided to travel to Florida and other Southern states in the summer of 1964 to participate in the Civil Rights struggle. The purpose of their trip was to forge discussions between white politicians, ministers, educators, and African American community and religious leaders about how to desegregate local businesses and integrate local restaurants.

I was particularly impressed since even though this group of largely white, privileged students had not experienced the injustices of segregation, they were willing to put themselves in harm's way for a noble cause. I didn't believe any harm would come to them because, naively, I still thought everybody in the United States had a right to work for a just cause. Of course, I was wrong. For their efforts to desegregate local businesses in St. Augustine, Florida, three Dartmouth college students spent some time in its jail. My mother was the treasurer of a fund that raised money for their bail.

Our activities weren't too popular with Dartmouth's predominantly conservative college student population. Several of them began to organize and campaign around the notion that we were part of an underground communist conspiracy intending to take over the country. I learned that during the 1950s, and still in the 1960s, there were many militias around the country spouting the same thing. For me, this was exactly the opposite of what we were trying to accomplish, which was to support legislation like the Civil Rights Act of 1964.

In the mid-1960s, the Vietnam civil war was becoming a concern on college campuses in the United States since it meant more graduates were going to be drafted and sent to fight, and perhaps to die, in Vietnam. U.S. involvement in that conflict began after the Geneva Convention of 1954, and slowly but steadily increased until it became a full-fledged war around 1965. Although Vietnam scheduled presidential elections for 1956, 1958, and 1960, all were postponed because, according to U.S. government officials, the "correct" person wouldn't win those elections.

Although the Vietnam War remained extremely popular among large segments of the U.S. population, anti-war sentiment in the United States was growing. In Hanover, many of those who organized against U.S. involvement in Southeast Asia were the same as those who were active in the Civil Rights movement. I found out that, while both efforts were about civil rights, organizing and campaigning against a faraway war was more difficult because there was very little information available about it, except for the often-incorrect tally of the dead.

* * *

PROTESTING WALLACE

I attended my first political demonstration against a candidate running for the nomination of a national political party in 1967 when the country was gearing up for the 1968 presidential election. The Republican Party had its standard bearer, Richard Nixon, running to be its candidate for president. Although everyone expected the Democratic Party to nominate Lyndon Johnson, Governor George Wallace was, thus far, the only other person who had declared his candidacy for the Democratic nomination. Wallace, the governor of Alabama, was an ardent advocate of segregation, who, on January 13, 1963, exclaimed during his inaugural gubernatorial address, "Segregation now, segregation tomorrow, segregation forever." Half a year later, he blocked two African American students from entering the University of Alabama campus, although a federal judge had ordered the state to admit them.

The *Dartmouth D*, the Dartmouth student newspaper known primarily for its conservative views, invited Wallace to speak at Webster Hall on the evening of May 3, 1967, probably to stir up liberal unease. The invitation angered many people who were associated with the college, as well as those who had no association with it. What was to be done? Nobody, to my knowledge questioned Wallace's right to speak. We did question, however, why anyone, except perhaps another segregationist, would want to listen to his rantings.

Many groups on and off campus organized to discuss these issues and how we could show our disdain for Wallace's beliefs and actions. My father, mother, and I joined a rather eclectic group of Dartmouth faculty and students at the Department of Asian Studies. The most widely known person in the group, both on campus, and probably to the federal government, was Professor Jonathan Mersky, who was famously known for his overwhelming desire to meet Ho Chi Minh. Mersky had traveled on a cargo ship to the harbor near Hanoi, the capital of North Vietnam, and tried to swim to shore, when the North Vietnamese refused to allow him to enter the country. He was plucked from the water by Vietnamese fisherman and put back on the ship.

At our first meeting, the U.S. Constitution was clearly on everyone's mind. If the First Amendment applied to this case, didn't Wallace have the right to give his speech? And, if so, did we have an equal right to show our disdain for his views? Some advocated that we should attend silently and then, at one point, we should all get up and leave. Others thought that we should be more assertive. All agreed that the best approach was to be nonviolent. We also wanted to act in concert as one group because the protest wouldn't be effective otherwise. After many meetings and phone calls, we decided on a plan of action. We would go to the meeting and not say a word until Wallace spewed his segregation rhetoric. Then we would talk back to him from the audience. In addition, to show our disgust with his views, each of us would wear a white sheet with the question, "Would you let Wallace marry your sister?" written in red paint across the front. We would not wear hoods.

When I entered the auditorium at Webster Hall with my group, I noticed that all the seats were taken, so I stood against the back wall of the auditorium close to an exit. I was glad that protesters far outnumbered the more conservative audience members. The person who introduced Wallace admonished us not to disrupt his speech. When Wallace came out, he opened by saying, "Now, if you listen to me, and I listen to you, we can communicate." Aside from the fact that the setting was not conducive to the discussion he proposed, his message was that integration was anti-Christian and the United States had to remain a white nation. Then, and only then, did people start yelling.

I had my own problems to deal with. I wasn't yelling or creating any other form of nuisance. However, just before the yelling began, one of George Wallace's Alabama state trooper bodyguards came up to me and said, in a rather stern and self-righteous voice, "Son, take off that sheet!"

I replied, "No," and turned around to watch the commotion in front of me.

With contempt in his eyes, he said, "Son, I'm going to say this one more time. Take off that sheet. Now! Or I will throw you out of the auditorium."

I turned to him and said, "You're an Alabama cop and you have no jurisdiction in New Hampshire, so get away from me and leave me alone."

He was furious, but it was true, he had no authority in this state. He did go away but he obviously told a New Hampshire state trooper who then told me, "Son, you better take off the sheet or I am going to have to take you out of here."

I said, "I have a right to express myself in any way that I want as long as I am doing so in a nonviolent way, Wallace is advocating violence, which is illegal."

He also walked away, but soon a Hanover police officer came over and said, "Henry, take off the sheet or you will have to leave." I guess I had a reputation.

I said, "No, I am not taking the sheet off and I'm not leaving the hall." He then asked another cop to help him escort me off the premises. But, instead of walking out, I sat down on the floor and wouldn't get up. They had to carry me out. There were many others who had already been asked to leave the hall and were listening to the happenings over WDCR, Dartmouth's radio station, which was broadcasting the speech.

I don't know what happened inside, but at one point a radio announcer said that Wallace had stopped talking and was leaving the stage with his notes under his arm. Everyone knew that he was supposed to spend the night at the Hanover Inn, but he decided instead that it would be safer for him to spend the night in Concord, New Hampshire's capital, about an hour's drive away. Neither the Dartmouth powers that be, from the president down, or the residents of Hanover thought very highly of our intervention. Most press accounts incorrectly admonished the protesters for trampling on Wallace's right to free speech.

* * *

DRAFT BOARD

In February 1971, nearly four years after graduating from high school, I received an invitation from the Selective Service Board to report on April 3 for a physical examination at the military recruitment office on Elm Street in Woodstock, Vermont. The purpose was to determine whether I was physically and mentally fit to be drafted and, perhaps, sent to fight in Vietnam. I didn't think that there was any possibility in hell that they would accept me into the army, but I wouldn't miss the opportunity to report for the physical if you paid me. The draft physical would provide me with firsthand knowledge of what I had only heard about on Arlo Guthrie's album *Alice's Restaurant* and seen in the movie based on it. It would also provide yet another opportunity to show my disdain for the conflict in Vietnam, and I relished the thought of saying this to someone in the military. I was excited to go to the draft board and do my civic duty!

Since my legal residence was in Norwich, it was possible for me to register for the military draft in Vermont rather than New York. This location was advantageous since there were not very many people drafted from Vermont because of its small population. Or, maybe droves of people from this very conservative state might have volunteered to enter the military. I don't know. All I knew was that it was less likely that the military would select someone from a rural state, such as Vermont, than an urban one, such as New York. In any case, it was most likely the military wouldn't have drafted me in any state under any conditions. My parents had moved to New York City by this time, so on April 3rd, I drove the family station wagon to Woodstock.

After I parked almost directly in front of the army recruitment office, I took my duffle bag and walked up the stairs to the office where the army officer behind the entrance desk gave me a quizzical look and asked, "What are you doing here?"

I said, "I received a letter telling me to report here for my physical. My draft lottery number is 42."

"Let me see the letter you received."

I reached into my pocket, withdrew the invitation and gave it to him. He read it, pondered for a moment, frowned, and said, "Wait here." I guess he was thinking that, given my physical appearance, it would be a waste of their precious time.

He took the letter, walked down the hallway, went into an office, and five minutes later came back and said, "Well, I guess you should take the physical. We are going to wait until 3:30 for everyone to get here and then we will drive everyone by bus to Manchester, New Hampshire, where there will be a day and a half of tests. Along the way, we will pick up people from other towns. Have a seat."

When the bus finally left, it picked up other unlucky people from towns along the route until we arrived at the Army Induction Center in Manchester. The 50 of us on the bus were divided into two groups. One group was going to have physicals that day and the other was going to take what they called, the "mental test." On the morning of the second day, the groups would switch. The group I was assigned to was going to be given the mental test that afternoon. The test was similar to the high school standardized PSAT test, except it was much simpler and lasted only about an hour. I was able to complete the test in a half hour because it was ludicrously easy. In my mind, it didn't measure very much.

During the two hours after the test, we filled out forms that made sure we were not undesirables, or, in other words, right-wing, communist, fascist, pinko bastards. A section of one of the forms had a list of more than 200 organizations that we were supposed to review and put a checkmark next to any we belonged to. I carefully and slowly read each item on the list so that I did not overlook any by mistake and then raised my hand.

The officer said, "Yes, Mr. Silvert, what can I do for you?'

"I am wondering about this list of organizations. I notice that the Ku Klux Klan of New Jersey is on the list, but the Ku Klux Klan of Alabama is not. Could you tell me why it is not listed?"

"I really don't know. Is it important?"

"I'm wondering whether the government thinks that any branches of the KKK are acceptable?"

"I don't know. Do you have any other questions?"

"Yes, I do. I see that the Socialist Party is on the list. Is this Michael Harrington's Socialist Party which is part of the Democratic Party or the Socialist Party of America?"

"I haven't any idea."

"Then I cannot sign my name to something that I am not sure about."

"Well son, you have certainly wasted our precious time with all these questions. Just place an X instead of your signature and I will witness it."

Hesitatingly, I put an X on the line where my signature should have been, and he came over, witnessed the X, and went back to his desk. I asked him why he accepted my X, and he told me that since my name was on other places in the forms, it didn't really matter. His reply didn't make me feel so good.

As soon as he sat down, I raised my hand again. Sounding a little irritated he asked, "What can I do for you now?" I just stood up and started singing Phil Ochs's *The Draft Dodger Rag*. The song is about the many reasons that the military might not want to accept the singer into its ranks of soldiers.

He stopped me before I started the second verse and said again, "You are wasting everybody's time. Just sit down and let us finish."

But I did not sit down. I kept on singing the other verses. And when I finished, I sat down, satisfied, with a big grin on my face.

The next morning, my group went into a large room. We were told to form a semi-circle and drop our shorts for our physical exam. I wasn't a happy camper doing this. Then each of us, separately this time, had to go into the psychiatrist's office to see whether our psyche was good enough to be drafted. When it was my turn, I went in and sat in a chair while he reviewed my chart. He didn't examine me at all but just looked at me and asked, "Why are you causing so much trouble?"

I said, "Because I don't think that what we are doing in Southeast Asia is justified, and it is my duty, as a citizen of this country, to let people know how I feel."

"Not everyone agrees with you."

"That's true, but there are also many people in this country and around the world who do agree with me. But, if you or somebody else doesn't agree with us, that's good. We can speak and debate the issue, and, by doing this, we can better understand each other's points of view. But this is not happening right now, and we need a dialogue. The only response that I've been getting here is, you're wasting our time. That's wrong, I'm not wasting anyone's time."

"Perhaps that is a good way of looking at things. In any event, congratulations, here is your 4F. Did you have any doubt that you were not going to be drafted?"

"No, I didn't but I did receive instructions to report for the physical."

Only one person in the entire group of the 50 people was deemed to be healthy enough for military duty. While I am sure that several others wanted to be accepted into the army, they were denied for several reasons including sleepwalking and having holes in their eardrums.

* * *

MORRIE: FALLING IN LOVE

I fell in love with my wife Morrie the first time I saw her. The gleam in her eyes, the swagger in her step, the ease of her conversation! I was tantalized. Yet, I thought that if I had any chance with her at all, I had to play it cool. I met her at a demonstration against the reinstatement of the military draft on July 21, 1979. It was a sweltering day. I was talking to Ed, an old family friend, in the middle of Broadway's three uptown lanes of traffic at 74th Street, in front of the Beacon Theater, when a beautiful woman, wearing blue shorts and a red top walked up to Ed and asked, "Hi Ed, what are you all doing here?"

Ed introduced us and told her we were there to demonstrate against President Carter's mandate that all 18-year olds register for the military draft. Ben, one of Ed's sons, had helped organize the demonstration. He suggested that she join us.

Morrie said that, she was on her way to drop off her shoes at Angelo's Shoe Repair and then had to prepare for her clarinet lesson the next day but that she'd stop by on her way back.

Ed explained to me that he and his wife Ruth, first met Morrie through mutual friends and had offered to let her live with them when she had come to the city from Chevy Chase, Maryland, to study with Leon Russianoff, a well-known clarinet teacher. She now lived in a building on the corner of Broadway and 79th Street.

Just before I met Morrie, I had started violin lessons yet again, at the Third Street Music School on 11th Street, and suddenly I was meeting musicians, at odd places like coffee shops and chess clubs, who were studying piano, violin, cello, or some other instrument at various music conservatories around the city. They were serious musicians, studying to be professionals, going to exotic music schools such as Juilliard, Mannes, and the Manhattan School of Music and, although I'd never heard them play, I envied their abilities. Now, I'd met a musician in a totally different environment, and I wondered how to make an impression!

When Morrie returned, I was deep in conversation in Spanish with a drunk Cuban who had approached me and, while waving a bottle of whiskey and slurring his words, was telling me that he wanted to tell the demonstrators they were all a bunch of dirty communist agents and should go back to the Soviet Union where they came from. Calmly, I suggested that he could do this better from the podium two blocks away. I escorted him there and made sure that the organizers knew what he wanted. To be honest, my main intention was to get him far enough away from where we were standing so he would not be able to find his way back to us. I raced back to Ed and Morrie and never saw the drunk Cuban again. Morrie later told me that she was very impressed by my tolerance with the man.

When the rally ended, Ed invited us to have dinner with Ruth and him at their apartment. I immediately accepted but Morrie demurred a bit saying that she really had to practice. Ed suggested that on the way she could pick up her clarinet so she could practice after dinner at their place. Maybe this was my chance to talk with Morrie. For me, the dinner was tasteless and nearly inedible, it was a Pritikin meal because Ed had a heart condition, and this is what they usually ate. Ruth was very interested to know how Morrie's music and my dissertation were progressing. After dinner, Morrie went into the front bedroom and practiced for a half-hour.

Later, as Morrie and I were walking back to 79th Street, I reached out to hold her hand while we were crossing Amsterdam Avenue. We walked hand in hand to her apartment building. I felt so happy! I didn't want the night to end. I suggested we sit on a bench in the median between the uptown and downtown lanes of Broadway to continue our conversation. That suggestion didn't go over too well because it was really hot and very late, but we exchanged telephone numbers before I went down to the subway station. When I called her the next evening, we decided to meet at my apartment, in the West Village, and then go to a nearby movie on Thursday.

I lived in a university-subsidized studio apartment on Bleecker Street. The movie was playing at a theater, which was about a 15-minute walk away. I had sparsely furnished my studio because I wanted to give myself a feeling of spaciousness. All of the furniture in the room was placed around the perimeter. I had a double bed, a brown rug, and two diagonally placed chairs at both ends of the rug facing the bed in one section of the room. My desk and dining room table with three chairs completed the other section.

I was so nervous on Wednesday night that I didn't get much sleep. I didn't want to screw up the date. I spent most of the day on Thursday at the New York University library. However, by 3:30 that afternoon, I was so tired that I went back to my apartment to lay down for a bit. I must have dozed off because the next thing I heard was the doorman ringing the buzzer letting me know that I had a guest. I frantically searched the apartment for my glasses but couldn't find them before Morrie rang the doorbell. The first thing that I said upon opening the door was, "Hi, Morrie. Can you help me find my glasses?" That night was the beginning of, what Chileans call, *pololeando*, or falling in love.

Our courtship was filled with unanticipated events like that night, which we now look back on with amusement. One time when Morrie's father, Martin, was in town, I offered to let him sleep on an extra bed. I had met some of my undergraduate roommates for drinks that night at the Algonquin Hotel. When I returned home, I tried to sit down on a chair but promptly tumbled to the floor because I was so drunk. Morrie was furious because she thought that her father wouldn't approve, but Martin stood up for me! I didn't understand why he did this at the time, but Morrie told me later he admired my rebellious spirit.

After Morrie moved into my studio, our neighbor across the hall, a single mother with a preadolescent son, complained there was too much noise coming from our apartment and loudly asked Morrie to practice somewhere else. Apparently, the walls were paper thin. We anticipated a note from the building manager saying that the music was too loud. However, later, when we heard her son playing his trombone, we knew that all was well. Her son had been inspired by the music!

Morrie and me at Café de Flore, Paris. France

Another time we were driving a borrowed car back from an anti-nuclear demonstration in Washington, D.C., when its engine block fell onto the road and we coasted to the shoulder. I got out of the car and started waving my arms frantically in the hopes that someone would stop. Five minutes later, two men in a pickup truck pulled up and asked where we were going. When we told them that we were headed to Manhattan, they said they could take us as far as Secaucus, New Jersey, where they lived. After they hitched our car to the back of the truck, Morrie climbed on my lap and the four of us set off. We told them that we only had $10, but if they gave us their address, we would be glad to send them more money to cover the expense. As we got closer to Secaucus, however, they decided that they would take us into Manhattan.

They dropped us in front of our apartment building and wouldn't accept any money. Perhaps it was just luck that they were so kind. I think that it was fate.

A little less than three years after we met, Morrie and I were married at a courthouse in Rockville, Maryland. Before the big day, Morrie went to Chevy Chase, Maryland, where her father lived, to prepare for the wedding reception. My family's plans to drive together in my mother's car hit a snag when her car was impounded because she had too many unpaid parking tickets. We ended up driving down in a rented car. As I was checking in at the courthouse, my love, the most beautiful, considerate, sensual woman I had ever met, came over and gave me kiss just before we were married.

EPILOGUE

The indelible event of the Mexican accident created an identity that could only be ameliorated, but never forgotten. The accident has always, whether consciously or unconsciously, influenced everything I've done. I will always have fond memories of relearning everything again after the accident, but, likewise, I will never forget the difficulty I experienced doing so. My parents continually provided me with the belief, the encouragement, and the vision that I could overcome the steepest of obstacles. While my mother passed her stubbornness and talent for self-advocacy on to me, she also taught me how to think critically. Not only about big issues like civil rights, equality, and war but also about the small things like communicating with friends and neighbors. My father gave me the patience and the wisdom I needed to learn about personal and social issues, but he also provided the space I needed to find my own way to address these issues. Both of my parents were ready to help me whenever I needed them, and my brothers always provided me with a source of friendly competition.

Writing this memoir has forced me to revisit some of the darkest times in my life so that I could make sense of my thoughts and behaviors today. This has been a complicated process. My social scientific background would suggest that if memories are interpretations of past events informed by present thoughts and behaviors, predictions of future events and behaviors would also be based on our understandings of the past. In this sense, the best prediction of a person's future is for it to be the continuation of their past experiences and behaviors unless there is an intervening traumatic and indelible event. In my case, the intervening event was my Mexican accident because, for a time, it wiped out my past, forcing me to start the learning process over again in its entirety. I don't know for sure if I would have developed the ideas that I have if I hadn't been in the accident. I certainly would have avoided the anguish and physical and mental challenges. I will also never know whether the accident promoted my sense of optimism or if it was my natural predisposition to view things this way. Whatever the cause, the care of my family and others certainly paved the path for me to be so positive. The kindness of friends and strangers in my unconsciousness and semi-consciousness states just after the accident may also have imbued a sense of optimism. I will never truly know the definitive role each of these factors may have played. What I do know, however, is that the kindness of those around me has helped to shape how I view others and understand events occurring throughout the world. This understanding has helped me create the invisible shield that protects me from the naysayers and those that would harm me. In the end, I think that it is my persistence and the support of my family and friends that have strengthened my innate optimism.

ACKNOWLEDGEMENTS

First and foremost, I would like to thank my wife Morrie for her continued encouragement, support and interest during the writing and rewriting of this memoir. Comments from my brothers Benjie and Ali were instrumental in confirming the chronology of our family's history. Joel and Betty Jutkowitz provided much needed details of the accident. I would also like to give a big thank you to Timothy Dennison for his insights on structure and help in organizing and completing the manuscript. Abby Corsun Sims deserves a special thanks for her insightful editorial suggestions. Thanks to Cynthia Holden for her insights into book cover design. Thanks to Salvatore Vitale and Wanda Hall who gave me much needed feedback on early drafts of the manuscript. A thank you goes to Robert Cohen who provided valuable thoughts on memoir structure. Finally, my appreciation to Ina Hillebrandt for her valuable feedback.

ABOUT THE AUTHOR

Henry M. Silvert, Ph.D., was born in Philadelphia in 1948, did his undergraduate (1967-1971) and doctoral studies (1976-1985) at New York University, and read for a Bachelor of Philosophy degree in Latin American area studies at the University of Oxford (1971-1974). He spent his childhood years in New Orleans, Guatemala City, Mexico City, Santiago, and Buenos Aires, and lived in Hanover, New Hampshire, and Norwich, Vermont as a teenager. As a survey associate and statistician, Dr. Silvert worked at The Conference Board, where he co-authored several reports regarding business matters, for 23 years. He has also worked on projects addressing, among other topics, childhood hunger, drug use, and the HIV/AIDS epidemic and gave presentations at conferences on Chile's return to democratic practices. Dr. Silvert has been a visiting professor at The Colegio de Mexico, where he taught comparative politics of Latin America, and an adjunct professor of sociology at various colleges and universities in New York City.